The Magic Money Tree
and Other Economic Tales

Comparative Political Economy

Series Editor: Erik Jones

A major new series exploring contemporary issues in comparative political economy. Pluralistic in approach, the books offer original, theoretically informed analyses of the interaction between politics and economics, and explore the implications for policy at the regional, national and supranational levels.

PUBLISHED

*Central Bank Independence
and the Future of the Euro*
Panicos Demetriades

Europe and Northern Ireland's Future
Mary C. Murphy

The Magic Money Tree and Other Economic Tales
Lorenzo Forni

A Modern Migration Theory
Peo Hansen

The Magic Money Tree and Other Economic Tales

Lorenzo Forni

agenda
publishing

First published in 2021 by Agenda Publishing

Agenda Publishing Limited
The Core
Bath Lane
Newcastle Helix
Newcastle upon Tyne
NE4 5TF

www.agendapub.com

ISBN 978-1-78821-364-6 (hardcover)
ISBN 978-1-78821-365-3 (paperback)

British Library Cataloguing-in-Publication Data
A catalogue record for this book is
available from the British Library

Typeset by Patty Rennie

Printed and bound in the UK by TJ Books

Contents

Acknowledgements

I have written this book to share with readers some of the lessons about the functioning of economic systems that I have learned over the years by studying and applying the tools and concepts of macroeconomics. I am grateful to several institutions where I have worked and gained this experience. They include the Bank of Italy, the International Monetary Fund, the University of Padua and Prometeia Associazione. Over this time, I have had the good fortune to work alongside many outstanding economists and to be exposed to many different points of view, which have helped shape my views on the topics I discuss in this text. To all of these people, I extend special thanks.

My primary motivation for writing this book is that, all too often, economic policy seems to do harm and impose unnecessary costs on populations of many different countries. These costs result in the waste of scarce resources, which could have been used more productively – to alleviate the suffering and deprivation of the most vulnerable social groups and, more generally, to contribute to the broader well-being of the entire national community. This damage is almost always due to poor economic policy choices based on distorted beliefs about how national economies work. In this book, I try to explain why we all might be better off if we were able to rid ourselves of these distorted views and agree about what is important.

Introduction:
pandemic economics

The size of the recession caused by Covid-19 is changing the way economists and policy-makers think about economic policy. The first few months of 2020 saw many economic policy boundaries being breached. In the space of a few months, the Federal Reserve, which is responsible for US monetary policy, almost doubled the value of its balance sheet assets, from about $4 trillion to $7.5 trillion, through a record issuing of trillions of dollars and, for the first time, direct lending to the private sector through the Main Street Lending Program. Before the pandemic, the Fed lent only to the banking system. In the UK, the Bank of England opened up a direct credit line to the UK Treasury, disregarding concerns over monetary financing of the government budget, actions historically perceived as very risky for central bank independence and, therefore, for the control of inflation.

These are just two examples that form part of a more general trend, in which the unprecedented economic crisis brought about by the pandemic has resulted in central banks intervening assertively with seeming little concern about whether their actions were risking financial soundness and might affect their ability to control inflation. In other words, these actions would seem to threaten the central banks' independence and even their very existence. The interventions have been enabled by continued low levels of inflation that have persisted over many years, and which have been exacerbated further by the pandemic.

The ability of central banks to act forcefully – a luxury not afforded to central banks in many emerging economies – has emboldened those who support the idea that central bank printing presses should run to finance government spending, as the supporters of modern monetary theory and certain politicians have claimed. Recently, many governments have benefited from the exceptional support offered by their central bank in the purchase of trillions of government bonds, enabling them to offer unprecedented fiscal support to the economy. It is estimated that the US budget deficit in 2020 will be the highest in its post-war history at close to 15 per cent of GDP. Australia, Germany, Japan and other countries are predicted to reach similar deficit levels.

It would seem that economic policy has no boundaries, which is a convenient assumption. If economic agents believe that money can be printed endlessly and that public spending has no limits, then they will feel confident about a recovery from the economic troubles induced by the pandemic. In addition, politicians can feel more relaxed in the context of seemingly unlimited borrowing and spending, which, in turn, will maintain their public support even in the most difficult economic environment. Also, most economists agree that a forceful policy response and some overlooking of the rules that have guaranteed macro stability in advanced economies over the past 30 years, is the appropriate response to the economic collapse caused by the pandemic.

And so it would seem that, in terms of economic policy, we are entering a new world. Can we relegate to history the ideas that printing money leads to inflation, that central banks should be independent, and that high public debt should scare investors and could lead to crisis? Is it the case that the main tenets held by economists and policy-makers over the previous 30 years were no more than intellectual constructs with no real hold?

What I shall argue in this book is that the main principles of economics remain unchanged; it is only the circumstances in which they operate that are currently different. After we have emerged from the pandemic-induced recession, the usual problems will return to haunt us. During the worst months of the pandemic, quite rightly, a consensus emerged between politicians and economists that fiscal and monetary policies should be assertive. However, traditionally, the two are in different camps and it will not be long before entrenched divisions about the proper course of economic policy will re-emerge.

Before the pandemic, it was normal for economists to complain about many of the economic policy measures being proposed or adopted by politicians. In the United States, winners of the Nobel prize for economics have

3

openly and harshly criticized the economic policy choices of the Trump administration and in the UK, before the 2016 referendum on UK membership of the European Union, many economists and the governor of the Bank of England were warning the UK government about the risks and likely costs of Brexit. In Italy in the past few years ambiguity has prevailed among government representatives regarding some fundamental choices such as commitment to the euro and reduction of public debt. Similar conflicts can be seen in many emerging economies, such as Argentina and Lebanon that are suffering deep crises. Fortunately, in other parts of the world, the economist–politician conflict is less extreme.

Traditionally, politicians are typically focused on their re-election chances, and therefore, on spending and giving away tax breaks, more than on balancing the books. They do not want or are unable to take account of the macroeconomic compatibility of their choices, whereas economists focus primarily on this aspect. In economist jargon, there is no such thing as a free lunch; in other words, everything comes at a price and nothing is created from nothing. This adage says a lot about how economists think. Economics, in fact, is characterized by the study of how to obtain the best possible results from scarce resources, that is, how to maximize an objective function given the constraints on what can be achieved. One point on which all economists would agree, therefore, is the fact that constraints exist – we will call them budget constraints – that must be respected. Economists might disagree about everything else, but on the need to include budgetary constraints in economic reasoning there is consensus.

However, politicians tend not to want to respect budgetary constraints. For them, the temptation to spend in order to buy consensus, with no one footing the bill, is strong, and as strong is the temptation to make others pay for their past excesses. The willingness of politicians to meet the growing demands for voter protection pushes them to promise and, sometimes, to implement policies that economists often consider ineffective and unsustainable in the medium to long term. In some cases, politicians make these choices knowing that they will involve costs in the medium term; in others, they are convinced that, despite the criticism they attract from economists, these are the right policies.

This book supports the thesis that there is a fundamental principle in economics that must always be respected and that can be appreciated with a minimum of application and common sense. This principle is that budgetary constraints must be respected in one way or another and that they determine the set of policies that can be considered sustainable. Indeed, there is no such thing as pandemic economics, there is only economics!

Not infrequently, and as I shall discuss more extensively below, certain unsustainable policies have been implemented in the attempt to create more wealth and greater well-being, so that voters, as far as possible, are satisfied. However, often, the politicians' horizon is short – extending to the next elections – and, therefore, they may be interested in supporting the economy only in the short term, without regard to whether the policies adopted are appropriate for the medium to long term. However, and this is a fundamental point, unsustainable macroeconomic policies sooner or later lead to crisis. Crises manifest themselves as more or less long and deep recessions, in which past excesses are corrected and citizens are called on to pay for them. If fiscal policy distributes resources that have not been produced, if a country spends more than it produces, in the end, someone has to pay for it: in short, sooner or later the budgetary constraint takes over. This leaves the question of who *should* pay, because in the distribution of the burden there is some leeway.

Obviously, in real life, things are complicated. It is often not straightforward to assess whether the policies introduced by the policy-makers are or are not sustainable. In some cases, the reality is extremely complex and it can be difficult to disentangle the facts to understand the real impact of the measures being adopted and, therefore, to assign responsibility for the economic crisis. The difficulty is linked, clearly, to the fact that there is no counterfactual, that is, we do not know what would have happened had certain policies not been implemented and had different choices been made. Even if we are able to anticipate events with reasonable certainty or if we are really convinced that the policy-makers' actions have contributed to an unsustainable situation, it can be difficult to determine whether the decision-makers were acting in good or bad faith. That is, whether they were aware of the risks to which they were exposing their country by their particular choice. Also, because macroeconomic sustainability is never certain, much depends on how events unfold. Unsustainable situations sometimes do not emerge for many years, for example, if there is a particularly favourable external economic environment.

So, there are many difficulties in trying to interpret politicians' actions. However, in many cases, and especially if the crisis is particularly severe, it is not difficult to identify the underlying reasons. These almost always are related to the persistent economic policy "errors" committed by policy-makers in the years preceding the crisis. By errors, I mean the inability of decision-makers to see or to admit that the policies proposed were unsustainable and, sooner or later, would have negative consequences. In short, despite the uncertainties and some past mistakes, economists tend to see more clearly than many politicians the risks of policies that do not take due account of the budget constraint.

The Covid-19 pandemic has pushed many countries a step closer to economic crisis and, while the economic policy response has been forceful, it has led to substantially higher public debt and significantly weaker central bank balance sheets. The latter effect is due to the central banks' interventions in the face of the crisis, and their purchase of large amounts of government and private bonds, which are linked to sizeable risks. It is more than possible that they will have to weather losses related to some of these assets.

During the deep recession that has characterized the peaks of the pandemic, economists and politicians have found some common ground and agreed about the need for large fiscal relief and monetary accommodations. However, as economies recover, politicians will find it difficult to dismantle this fiscal support. Central banks will come under considerable pressure to continue to ease monetary conditions and keep their printing presses subordinate to the needs of the public budget. We are starting to see some of these effects already and economists are beginning to highlight the unsustainability of current courses of action. The clash between politicians and economists was temporarily put to rest by the pandemic, but is set to return – and to be even more divisive than before.

My aim in this book is to inform and to contribute to a better awareness of the importance of prudent and sustainable macroeconomic policies, that is, policies that are consistent with respect for budgetary constraints. I imagine that for the more sophisticated reader, the reasoning in this book might be considered straightforward; however, for many others, including many voters and politicians, it should be useful.

For clarity, the book is organized on two levels. Firstly, for each type of economic policy I deal with, and I will focus only on macroeconomic policies (i.e., monetary, fiscal, exchange rate and international trade policies), I provide a country example that I believe demonstrates the misuse of that specific policy and I explain some of its practical implications. The country examples are illustrative of the more general situation too and I am not seeking to blame any particular government. Secondly, following each policy and country case, I provide a description of the conceptual aspects useful to achieving a better understanding of the example I offer. I will try to explain why things did not go as the policy-makers of those countries perhaps expected or wanted. Of course, no single policy is adopted in isolation from other policies, and a country that tends to mismanage its monetary policy may also be more likely to mismanage other policies. However, for exposition purposes, I need to make some simplifications; I would ask for the reader's forbearance if, in some cases, I stylize realities that are much more complex. The appendix provides a brief and simplified description of budgetary constraints, with the help of symbols, sums and subtractions. To understand the arguments in the main part of the book, it is not strictly necessary to read this appendix, but it might be useful for those keen to obtain a deeper understanding of the functioning of macro-economic budget constraints and the interrelationships between them and economic trends.

Finally, a caveat. Although, the text might appear to be rather technical at times, I feel sure that anyone who reads it carefully will be able to follow my proposed reasoning. Most of the arguments I propose are based on common-sense reasoning and not cryptic and incomprehensible formulae. In short, those about to embark on this text may have to work at certain points, but I hope that they will be rewarded with a greater awareness about these important issues.

1

The clash between politicians and economists

"It will take a lot for people to get there, although I predict that a few years from now, when you ask people whether they voted Trump in 2016, the vast majority will say they didn't."

Paul Krugman, July 2018*

Paul Krugman, an economist with a career at the best universities, Nobel prize-winner, and one of the world's most famous and respected economists, has been one of President Trump's leading critics. Via Twitter (and his column in *The New York Times*) Krugman has not pulled his punches, taking on the president for his economic policy choices. Moreover, as an expert on international trade, Krugman has targeted Trump's protectionist proposals and

---

* On Twitter; https://twitter.com/paulkrugman/status/1023274059252092928.

measures. He has not been alone in his criticism, as most economists believe that the main measures adopted and proposed by the Trump administration have been wrong.

In fact, the Trump administration seems to have ignored all of the economists' suggestions. In 2018, it initiated a broad fiscal stimulus including tax cuts and spending increases, which made the US debt dynamic even more unsustainable than it was already. Trump launched a series of bilateral trade negotiations, threatening and implementing tariffs and other protectionist measures, when economic theory argues that what matters is the overall trade deficit (not the bilateral deficits) and that there are benefits from free trade. The insight that countries are better off exporting the products they are relatively good at producing while importing the others, dates back to the ideas of the British political economist David Ricardo (1772–1823).*

---

* Here is an example to explain Ricardo's idea, known to economists as the principle of comparative advantage. If a country is relatively more efficient at producing airplanes than cars, it should focus in producing airplanes and then trade them for cars. By not producing cars, the country could produce a good number of extra airplanes and then trade these additional airplanes for cars. Having a comparative advantage with respect to the trading partners in producing airplanes implies that the additional airplanes produced can be traded for a larger number of cars than those the country could have produced domestically by making fewer airplanes. Therefore, trade allows to increase the aggregate well-being of countries. Of course, when the country opens up to trade and – in our example – realizes it is better off to shut down the car industry, auto workers might be dismissed and therefore for them trade is not such a good deal. Indeed, as it is now widely accepted, trade can have negative distributive consequences.

Observing such a divergence between economists and politicians in the United States, one of the most developed countries in the world, makes one think. Is it possible that the president of the most powerful economy in the world would ground his policies in erroneous reasoning or data that do not exist? Or is it that economists are losing touch with reality and do not understand that their theories no longer work? Indeed, economists are not infallible. They were widely criticized for not having foreseen the financial crisis of 2008, epitomized by Queen Elizabeth's now infamous question, "Why did no one see it coming?" during a visit to the London School of Economics in 2008. They also failed to understand and anticipate the dissatisfaction of the American middle class that led to the election of Donald Trump. So, who has got it right? Krugman seems to be right that some American voters have changed their mind regarding Donald Trump, but the debate is open over whether his economic policies have been a fiasco or not. Certainly, they were based on premises that economists do not share.

To be clear, the conflict between politicians and economists is not only a fact of the United States. Without being exhaustive, a few other examples will help illustrate the issue. When the British decided to hold a referendum on their membership of the European Union (the famous Brexit), many economists and international institutions, including the International Monetary Fund (IMF 2016), predicted that a vote to leave would be detrimental to the British economy. Pro-Brexit campaigners criticized these predictions, believing that they were the result of political positions rather than objective analysis. Now, despite the fact that making predictions about Brexit, as events have shown, has been very difficult, it is undeniable that the economic situation in the UK has been negatively affected by the protracted process of exiting the European Union.

A particularly vivid example exists in the tense relations between politicians and economists in Italy. In 2018, an Italian government was formed that did not have a clear line on how to reduce the public debt which exceeded 130 per cent of gross domestic product (GDP). Furthermore, some politicians from majority parties called for the use of money (perhaps printed by an independent central bank outside the eurozone) to finance public spending. Many economists (certainly the ones who were not active in politics), if not most of them, have criticized these proposals as inappropriate, likely ineffective and having arisen from a misunderstanding of the basic mechanisms of economics. Although some of the politicians who held these positions have since changed their opinion, in Italy there remains a gap between the convictions of some politicians and those of most economists on such important issues. How is it possible that this "divergence" remains unresolved, that politicians cannot sit around a table with a representative sample of economists to find common ground? This book will deal with that question too.

Interestingly this conflict between politicians and economists has often been seen in many developing countries and in dictatorial regimes. In the latter, as we shall see, the conflict is peculiar because dictatorships do not need democratic legitimacy and can therefore afford choices that would not be possible in other countries. But in many emerging countries the conflict has been and is still ongoing. There was a long sequence of economic policy errors in various South American countries that led to public debt crises in the 1980s, just as there were the Asian and Russian crises of the late 1990s. The most emblematic case, with a long history in this regard, is that of Argentina, which within a few years of defaulting on its public debt in 2001, fell back into crisis in 2018 due to excessive foreign borrowing and had to seek help from the international community. All this despite the fact that economists had warned that the policies adopted in the years running up to the crisis risked leading the country into a crisis (e.g., IMF 2017). As a result, Argentina is still on its knees, stuck in a recession.

The point of view of politicians

"It's the economy, stupid!"

James Carville, Bill Clinton's advisor
in the 1992 presidential election.

The relationship between the economic performance of a country and its election results is widely debated, but there is a broad consensus that when the economy is going well, politicians who manage to take credit for it usually do better in elections. An idea that James Carville understood and used during Clinton's 1992 presidential election campaign. The relationship is complex for several reasons. Sometimes it is not easy to blame someone for economic trends. Things can go wrong because of an exogenous (or external) shock, such as an international recession, for which the politician at home has no responsibility. The Covid-19 pandemic is another example of an exogenous shock, although there has been a lot of discussion about how much to blame national leaders for the different national outcomes. Perceptions too are important.

Voters may have perceptions that are not fully in line with the facts and may therefore punish politicians even when things are not going so badly. For example, at the end of 2017 some polls in Italy reported that most respondents believed the economic crisis triggered by the European sovereign debt crisis of 2011–12 was at its peak, and that things would improve thereafter. In reality the Italian economy was in its fourth year of growth at the end of 2017. Probably the economic improvement had been too weak and insufficient to have had a practical impact on the everyday life of many voters. However, the fact remains that the perception was distorted and probably weighed on the electoral consensus of the government that had managed the economy in those years.

Attributing blame, for example, for the poor performance of the economy is less relevant when new candidates run for election, who cannot be held accountable for past performance, and who are free to make generous promises about future economic performance in order to win the voters' favour. Some voters may not give much credence to unbelievable promises made by politicians, but will still vote for those who make the promises that are most pleasing to them. By doing so, they minimize the probability that the promise of some other politician will be carried through. Should the desired politician then win the election, in the worst-case scenario nothing will happen and in the best case some advantage may be gained.

The fact remains that a successful economy helps the politicians in the consensus (Giuliani & Massari 2018). And it is quite intuitive that politicians have an interest in using the levers at their disposal in economic policy to stimulate the economy and appropriate the merits of its good performance. Certainly, with an eye to the next elections. A classic political move is to opt for a fiscal expansion to support economic activity in the run up to elections. Since the central banks of most countries have a large degree of independence, it is more difficult for politicians to affect monetary policy (in reality, as we shall see, in many countries politicians *are* able to intervene on that too). President Trump, for example, implemented a fiscal expansion between the end of 2017 and the beginning of 2018 hoping that its effects would materialize in time to be widely felt before the mid-term elections in November 2018. The fiscal relief measures of 2020, ahead of the November presidential elections, were the largest in postwar US history, and complemented by a very accommodative stance from the Fed, given the exceptional circumstances of the pandemic.

Obviously, the important horizon for politicians is the one that separates them from the next elections. And there is nothing wrong with wanting to stimulate the economy, if you do it in an effective and sustainable way. What is less justified are short-term stimuli that are unsustainable in the medium to long run and therefore, sooner or later, involve costs for the country and its citizens. It is like asking a marathon runner to sprint for the first few kilometres in order to make an excellent half-way time, at the cost of seeing the runner having to take a break later and perhaps even not finish the race.

But it is actually worse than that. Politicians often not only stimulate the economy with an eye to the next election, but as I shall argue later on, they also often do it in the wrong way. They frequently see or think they see an advantage in certain measures, without realizing that they are inappropriate measures and that they are likely to do more harm than anything else. A good example is the protectionist measures pursued by President Trump. By imposing tariffs on imports, Trump sought to reduce the purchase of foreign goods, protect domestic production of those goods on which he imposed tariffs, and in this way, contain the trade deficit. But what has actually happened is that the US's trading partners have taken similar measures in response, placing the US at the centre of a trade war in which its exports to some important trading partners are also subject to tariffs.

Another Italian example is the proposal for a strong fiscal expansion contained in the M5S and Lega 2018 government agreement, which was to prove counterproductive for a country that at the time had debt levels above 130 per cent. As soon as the programme was announced, the spread on Italian government bonds (i.e. the cost that the Italian state had to pay with respect to a similar bond that is considered safe, such as German government bonds) increased, imposing additional costs on the public purse. The increase in interest rates on government bonds is typically passed on to the rest of the economy (why lend to a private company at lower rates if one can get a higher rate by lending to the government?) with implications in terms of lower investment and economic growth. Therefore, just the announcement of plans for a strong fiscal expansion in a context where it may not be sustainable entails costs. We shall return to this issue later in the book.

Some might think that in reality politicians are not really interested in increasing economic growth per se, but only in favouring the social groups that support them or, even worse, their close friends. These different objectives are not in conflict. Of course, if I am a politician I can help my friends, but that will hardly be enough to win national elections. A more delicate question is that of favouring certain social groups over others. This typically happens when a government tries to introduce reforms with the aim of increasing the efficiency of the economic system. In doing so, in most cases, it will harm a few specific groups for the wider benefit of the community as a whole. From an electoral point of view, such a strategy may not pay off, because the groups adversely affected may team up to oppose the reform, while the beneficiaries may be widespread and unorganized and therefore politically less active. An alternative strategy might be to favour only certain social groups in order to build their loyalty to the government in office and to be sure of their support for the elections. The difficult part is doing this without harming other social groups as, for given resources, it simply means redistributing from one social group to another.

To take the US case again as an example, imposing tariffs on imports of iron and aluminium, as Trump did in 2018 to favour the US producers of these metals that were located mainly in areas that were the basis of his 2016 presidential victory, levies a cost on all US producers of other goods that use these metals as intermediate inputs. Therefore, the introduction of tariffs on metals may have brought Trump a few votes among the producers of these metals, but he lost them from those who buy these metals instead. In short, redistributive policies may not pay electorally.

That is why it is important to try to grow the economy, so as to have more resources to redistribute. Remaining with the example of duties on iron and aluminium, if, together with tariffs, a strong fiscal stimulus is introduced that makes the economy grow, as the Trump administration did at the end of 2017, the additional cost, in terms of higher metal prices, for those who use iron and aluminium as an intermediate input could be compensated, or maybe more than compensated, by the increased overall demand and likely demand for their products. As we shall see in the rest of this book, the world is full of examples of countries and governments in office that have used the levers of the economy to strengthen their leadership position.

The economists' point of view

"We must focus specifically on living standards and human, social and natural capital when we set targets and track progress. [...] But change of this scale requires us to look beyond three and four year electoral cycles."

Jacinda Ardern,
Financial Times, 21 January 2019

I am an economist, so I might be biased. Nevertheless, I will endeavour to give a balanced and dispassionate representation of what I believe to be the economy and its limitations. But to be clear, in this book, we are talking about only one part of economics, which deals with macroeconomic aggregates, because our main focus is economic policy. And within economic policy, I examine those main issues that invite public debates the most, namely fiscal policy (taxes, expenditure, public debt), monetary policy, exchange rate policy and trade policy.

I do not address, or only in passing, other policies, such as those on competition, market regulation, and education. These other policies are often referred to as supply-side policies, as opposed to demand-side ones. Most of the analysis in this book is focused on demand-side policies. In fact, as I will argue, politicians should most of the time focus their efforts on supply-side policies because they are the ones that can most elevate a country's productive capacity and growth potential.

Macroeconomic policies should be managed primarily with the aim of ensuring macroeconomic stability within which all other economic activities can safely take place and flourish, such as innovation, human capital accumulation and market regulation. The biggest mistake, as I shall argue in this book, is to think that budgetary and monetary policies can raise growth potential in a lasting way. Macroeconomic policies can and must stabilize fluctuations in the economic cycle, or help prevent and mitigate crises and recessions, thereby creating a stable environment within which longer-term investment can be conducted without the disruptions caused by continued uncertainty over aggregate activity. It is no surprise therefore that those policies have been deployed forcefully to counter the Covid-19 recession.

What needs to be done, described in this way, sounds simple. But stabilizing the economy or preventing crises is not an easy task: the financial crisis of 2008 is proof of this. Economists, and macroeconomists in particular, more than ten years later, are still soul-searching for not having predicted the crisis in advance and are still occupied in understanding why they were unable to anticipate it. In essence, critics have argued that economics is unable to make reliable forecasts (otherwise it would have sounded the alarm before 2008) because it uses erroneous or inaccurate models. It is not the purpose of this book to discuss the merits of these criticisms and the justifications that economists have proposed (see Rodrik 2015). My opinion, in short, is that the truth is somewhere between the two.

The models had limits that macroeconomists have been working on for years, but we are still far from a completely satisfactory solution.

What then remains of macroeconomics? From what I have written so far, the reader could be under the impression that macroeconomics is unreliable and therefore of little use. Nothing could be further from the truth. Even if the models are imperfect, and objectively making accurate forecasts is difficult, it is nevertheless my deep conviction, gained through years of experience in the field, that the fundamental principles of macroeconomics are more solid than ever, and it is on these principles that economic policy must be based.

What are these principles? The main one, which has a number of implications, is that budget constraints must be always respected, one way or another. Budgetary constraints operate at the level of the individual household, the state, and the country with regard to non-residents. The budgetary constraint of the individual household is familiar to us all and one we face every day. For the state it refers to the fact that if public expenditure exceeds revenue, a deficit is created, and therefore a debt, which to be repaid might require tax rises or expenditure cuts.* The

---

* Blanchard (2019) has reminded us that when the average cost of the debt (r) is below the rate of growth of the economy (g), therefore when $r - g < 0$, any fiscal deficit will lead to a stable level of public debt. This is a theoretical property of the debt dynamics, more than a prescription to run a large deficit. For example, if $(r - g) = -1$ per cent and the primary deficit is equal to 5 per cent of GDP, the debt/GDP level converges to a value of 500 per cent of GDP, hardly realistic.

trade constraint is similar: if we import more than we export, we are accumulating debt to non-residents, which sooner or later we will have to repay.

All these budgetary constraints, which are then inter-related, must be respected. That is, what is feasible in the economy is possible only if it meets the various budgetary constraints. Let us immediately clarify an important aspect, the budgetary constraint acts over time (it is "inter-temporal", as economists say). You can spend more than what you earn by getting into debt for a certain period of time, but sooner or later this must find an end. At a certain point, you will have to cut back on consumption to avoid piling up further debt.

As I will argue later, often the attempt by politicians to stimulate the economy is simply an attempt to escape the budgetary constraint, which is not possible. Only policies that comply with it are sustainable, and therefore only those policies give rise to stable configurations. The others inevitably lead, if not corrected, to crises. Now the reader may think that I am diminishing the role of macro-economics and economic policy too much. But in fact, if every time a policy is proposed, one were to ask what its implications for the budget constraint would be, we would already have made a lot of progress. If we all accepted the idea that the budgetary constraint exists and must be respected, many of the proposals made by politicians would immediately lose credibility.

At the heart of economic policy is, in essence, the assessment of how the introduction of a policy will act on the budgetary constraint over time and how this will ultimately be respected. The rest of this book addresses exactly this issue, with reference mainly to three policies: monetary policy, fiscal policy, and foreign exchange and trade policy. An important point that I will try to make clear is that when the policy-makers introduce a policy to stimulate the economy, they must pay attention to the two main budgetary constraints that affect a nation (the domestic and the external one), otherwise sooner or later there will be an economic crisis. As I shall argue, the economic crisis is nothing other than a way of restoring and satisfying, albeit often very expensively, the budgetary constraint.

In fact, economic crises are usually characterized by different combinations of output contraction, devaluations, inflation, and default on public debt. These elements ensure that in the end the budgetary constraints are satisfied. That is to say, the introduction of unsustainable policies, that is policies that violate the intertemporal budget constraint, inevitably leads to phenomena that restore its validity, even if in an extremely painful way: recessions and devaluations reduce imports and increase exports, leading to a trade surplus, and therefore help to satisfy the external budget constraint with foreign residents; inflation, often driven by currency devaluations, makes it possible to reduce the real value of public debt, effectively imposing a tax on its holders and helping to stabilize its dynamics;* and default is another way to

---

* Inflation reduces the purchasing power of money and also of
  government bonds, as they are generally defined in nominal terms.

devalue debts and restore the sustainability of the budget constraint.

Importantly, this type of adjustment usually weighs most on the weaker social classes and the working classes (see, among others, Ball *et al.* 2013). In recessions, marginal and less educated workers are the first to lose their jobs. In cases of sharp increases in inflation, it is the real incomes of employees and the purchasing power of households that are most affected. If the fiscal adjustment is achieved by defaulting on public debt, a large amount of household savings will go up in smoke. Only if the default refers to debt held by non-residents, then domestic costs may be contained, but even in these cases the working classes tends to bear most of the costs of adjustment, because default is usually accompanied by severe economic crises and austerity policies (Forni *et al.* 2020).

Unfortunately, politicians, even those who understand the consequences of unsustainable policies and who realize that at some point such policies should be reversed in order to respect the intertemporal budgetary constraint, may still have an interest in not changing course. Indeed, "course correction" often means introducing restrictive monetary and fiscal policies to ensure that the budget constraint can be met without facing a crisis. In fact, it often means reversing the policies previously promised and implemented, and therefore in a certain sense it means disavowing oneself and harming one's credibility. Moreover, such policies are typically unpopular and often require the government to make choices about which social groups should contribute most to the adjustment. Only in very cohesive societies (which are typically small countries with few ethnic, religious and cultural differences) can agreement be reached that all social groups contribute to adjustment. This was in some ways the case in the Baltic states (Estonia, Latvia and Lithuania) after the 2008 crisis, but it should be noted that the largest of these countries, Lithuania, only has about 3 million inhabitants.

Often, arriving at a crisis (of sovereign debt or foreign debt) is much more expensive from a social point of view, but it makes the problems "solve themselves", in the sense that it requires fewer discretionary choices on the part of policy-makers. Strong devaluation with inflation, for example, could be avoided at times, if the central bank raised interest rates significantly. But to do so would be to admit that an unsustainable policy had been conducted in the past and to attract criticism from voters for the decision to raise interest rates that impose costs on citizens. If, on the other hand, there is an exchange rate crisis, the resulting sharp rise in domestic inflation will achieve much of the correction needed to restore and meet the budgetary constraint. The domestic authorities will be able to say that they are not to blame, in the sense that the devaluation and ensuing inflation are not their choice but the result of the actions of some foreign speculator. History is full of such cases. We will delve further into details of these in the following chapters.

What do we mean by "budgetary constraints"?

"We must consult our means rather than our wishes."
George Washington, 1780

Before getting to the heart of the book, I would like to clarify what is meant by "budgetary constraint". It is natural to first think of the public budget constraint, but as we shall see, the concept extends far beyond that. The public budget constraint implies that, if a state spends more than it collects in taxes, it will have to cover the difference by borrowing. Obviously, this deficit can be financed with debt for a few years, perhaps even many years if it is not large, and in doing so it will accumulate. But sooner or later it will be necessary to correct the imbalance due to the fact that expenditures are higher than revenues. It will be necessary to reduce public expenditure or increase public revenue, or both, in such a way as to bring the public budget into surplus and thus make available those resources to start repaying and reducing the public debt.

It should be noted that the public budget constraint, as well as the other budgetary constraints we shall examine, are not substantially different from those we face in our everyday lives. As a family, we have income, typically income from work of the spouses and perhaps some return on savings invested in financial assets or real estate, and expenses, for housing (rent or mortgage), food and domestic utilities, and everything else including leisure. As a family, we know very well that we cannot constantly spend more than our income, first and foremost because the money in the current account would soon run out. We can afford something in excess via borrowing, for example we can buy a car via a car loan, but in this way we have to pay the instalments to pay off the debt incurred to buy the car. In short, families, as states, also have revenues, expenses and debt.

It can happen that there are imbalances in our family budget. For some reason, expenses may be higher than income for a period of time long enough to exhaust our savings and drain any cash in the bank account. When it gets to that point, all we have to do is to make a correction, that is either reduce our spending or try to increase our income. You can try to increase your debt, but typically for a family this is not easy.

The state faces a similar budgetary constraint. It is fortunate, however, that its "creditworthiness" is usually higher than households. This is because the state has the power to tax and so can get into debt knowing that in the future it can relatively easily increase its revenues by raising taxes. If it were otherwise we could not explain why many states have debts equal to or greater than 100 per cent of their gross domestic product, which is the income of a country. It is difficult for a family, and perhaps even for an entrepreneur, to have debts in excess of annual income or revenue without pledging some assets as collateral.

The fact remains that a state is subject to the budgetary

constraint. If it spends too much and accumulates debt, creditors may begin to have doubts as to whether it will be able to repay it. It is true that a state can enact laws to reduce expenditure and increase revenue, but there are limits within which it can do so. If taxes are already at very high levels, it will be difficult to raise them further. If the spending inefficiencies have already been reduced, all that remains is to cut programmes that are of value to the citizens and thus to face political opposition and weakening of consensus. If the economy is in recession or ailing, cutting spending and increasing revenue can further weaken economic activity. This could be reflected in the state budget, creating pressure for higher spending (e.g. unemployment benefits) or lower revenues (linked to the weak phase of the economy and economic activity). This is a significant difference between the households' and the state's budget constraints, as individual households cutting back on consumption generally does not have macroeconomic implications. The fact remains that, even for a state, there is a limit to how much it can get into debt.

Although the budgetary constraint of the state is perhaps the most obvious, another important budgetary constraint is the external one. While the state's budget constraint measures the relationship between the state and the private sector, in the sense, for example, that a state usually has as creditors both domestic residents and citizens of other countries (a country's government bonds are typically also sold abroad), a nation's external budget constraint measures a country's debt and credit relationship with foreign residents. For example, the external budget constraint measures whether a country's residents, including the public sector, consume foreign goods – i.e. imports, which need to be paid in foreign currency – to a greater extent than foreigners consume domestic goods – i.e. exports, which are mostly sold in foreign currency and are therefore a source of it. If the two amounts are more or less similar, residents as a whole will be able to use export earnings to pay for imports.

If, on the other hand, there is an imbalance, for example, residents import more than they export, the excess of imports would create a shortfall of foreign currency and would have to be paid for either by reducing domestic assets held abroad or by borrowing abroad. That is, a resident citizen can use export earnings to pay for imports, or pay with cash kept in foreign currency (for the sake of simplicity, an import from the United States to be paid in dollars), or finally incur a debt (in this example in dollars) to pay for the excess of imports. If there is a persistent imbalance in the foreign accounts, such that a country accumulates a significant level of foreign debt, this will have to be corrected sooner or later to allow the stabilization or repayment of the foreign debt. This basically means being subject to the external budget constraint.

It should be noted that all these budgetary constraints have an effect over time. That is, an imbalance – for example, higher public expenditure than revenue – will be manageable over a certain period of time, for example, through debt accumulation. The constraint will not become tight, in the sense of forcing a change of course, immediately. A country can accumulate debt for a while.

But eventually the imbalance has to be corrected. How long a country can go on accumulating debt depends very much on its history, the strength of its economy, and external circumstances, such as creditors' preferences.

There are other constraints that we shall discuss, which are generally to do with the budgetary constraints of companies and banks. These constraints operate in the same way because companies and banks also have revenue and expenditure. The income typically depends on the sale of goods and services produced, while the expenses are the operating expenses to run the business. These expenses obviously include interest charges on borrowed cash and cash equivalents. Companies and banks can also get into debt and usually do so. Companies can typically borrow from banks or issue bonds in the market, while banks get the liquidity from savers' deposits, and they can issue bonds in the market as well. For banks there is another type of loan, the one they can get from the central bank through monetary policy operations.

This brings us to the last budgetary constraint that we will discuss, which is that of the central bank. The central bank is an atypical entity because it has the capability of printing money. This might lead you to think that the budgetary constraint does not apply to the central bank. And apparently, there are people who believe this, namely supporters of modern monetary theory (MMT).* After all, a central bank can print as much money as it wants

---

* For primers on MMT see Wray (2015) and Kelton (2020).

and therefore there is no reason it will ever have to go into debt.

But the point is that a central bank needs to maintain a healthy balance sheet in order to be credible in controlling inflation. If there are upward price tensions, central banks have a limited number of options to deploy. They can mop-up liquidity by selling assets, or by paying a high interest rate on banks reserves (commercial banks' deposit with the central bank) in order to induce them to increase the liquidity deposited with the central bank. In both cases, the asset side of the central bank balance sheet has to be in the position to allow these operations to be sustained, possibly for a prolonged period of time. This implies that, ideally, the asset side has a monetary value close to the liability side (which is mainly comprised by money issued by the central bank) and that the returns on assets are sufficient to pay the high interests on reserves that may be required.

Moreover, there is no fundamental difference between financing public expenditures with debt or by printing money. The central bank is part of the state and therefore falls within its budget constraint. If it buys government bonds and issues money, the money bills issued are still liabilities of the state towards the money holders. Liabilities in the sense that agents will be able to use them to pay for current and future tax obligations. If the central bank pays interest on money holdings, money financing is not different from bond financing. If the central bank does not pay interest on money holdings, agents will resist exchanging government bonds for money and this will bring up the price of bonds. If the central bank keeps buying government bonds, as it has been the case in recent years, the price of bonds will soar and the interest rate paid on them will approach zero (or even go negative). At that point, again, there is no difference between bond and money financing, as neither pay interest. I'll come back to these issues in Chapter 4.

In short, our discussion of budgetary constraints will refer to all the constraints described so far. In the end, the budgetary constraint is what puts a brake on countries getting into debt indefinitely. We shall see that policymakers are either able to correct situations of persistent imbalance that lead to excessive debt, or push their countries into crisis and recession. Crises and recessions are traumatic ways of restoring the budgetary constraints. In one way or the other, the budget constraint must be met.

2

The magic potion of credit

"Long-term economic growth depends mainly on nonmonetary factors such as population growth and workforce participation, the skills and aptitudes of our workforce, the tools at their disposal, and the pace of technological advance."

Jerome Powell,
Chairman of the Federal Reserve*

I start by analysing monetary and credit policy, because, however unpalatable it may be, banks – or rather credit – are fundamental to the functioning of economic systems. National banking activity is controlled by a central bank, which regulates the liquidity in the economic system and,

---

* "The Economic Outlook and Monetary Policy", Remarks by Jerome H. Powell, Member Board of Governors of the Federal Reserve System at the Forecasters Club of New York Luncheon, New York, 22 February 2017; https://www.federalreserve.gov/newsevents/speech/powell20170222a.htm.

indirectly, the flow of credit. As a child, I was fascinated by the idea that "someone" had the power to print money. This someone is the central bank, which has the power, it seems, to create wealth out of nothing. It is no coincidence that the creation of value from nothing has fascinated over the years many politicians, and even the film industry, for example it is the focus of the successful Spanish television series *La casa de papel*, and the famous 1956 Italian movie about forgers *La banda degli onesti*.

Credit appears to have magical qualities because, by creating money, the central bank is able to provide liquidity that allows the high-street banks to lend to entrepreneurs and consumers. Leaving consumer credit aside for the moment, what is remarkable is that credit enables entrepreneurs to invest, create new products, develop new activities and increase production. However, there is no "magic potion", just the reality of the money printed by the central bank. This money that is created (printed) is used for central bank loans, which, eventually, must be repaid to the central bank.

The attraction of easy credit

To introduce the subject of credit, I will use the example of a small country that straddles northern Europe and Russia. What is interesting about this country is that it is one of the few in the world whose economy is still organized on a five-year plan and mostly follows the classic Soviet-style approach. In this system, the central bank is not independent and, thus, the political authorities directly control the management of credit. For the last 20 years, the country has often used credit to excess to support the national construction market and to make the economy grow. I will explain why this strategy did not have the effect desired by the country's leadership.

The country is Belarus, but I should make clear, first of all, that it is not an isolated case. There are other planned economies that attach great importance to the use of credit as an economic policy instrument. China is the largest and most successful state-run economy. Its economic policy relies on strong credit growth (Wolf 2018) to the extent that the recent huge growth of monetary indicators can be considered one of China's greatest vulnerabilities and worries many analysts (and economists!). We shall return to these aspects in Chapter 4. However, China is a large country, which makes it more difficult to isolate the impact of individual policies. Belarus operates in a similar way but is a smaller economy and, therefore, easier to understand.

I could have focused perhaps on a more developed country, but it would have been more difficult to explain its mechanisms. For example, before the financial crisis in 2008–09, Spain recorded a strong expansion of credit, channelled towards the real estate sector, resulting in all the problems with which we are now familiar (Lane 2012). The crisis was accompanied by excess credit in a large number of advanced countries, the most prominent being the United States and the United Kingdom. However, whereas in the cases of Spain, the US or the UK it would be difficult to argue that this excess credit was the result of a clear political plan, in Belarus, on the contrary, the country is by definition a planned economy. Therefore, using the example of Belarus to demonstrate leaders misusing economic levers simplifies matters.

Until a few years ago, construction was the fastest growing sector in Belarus, because the Central Bank of Belarus facilitated the granting of easy credit, which was used mainly by construction companies to build housing. Why was it focused mostly on this sector? For many firms, but especially building companies, it was easier to focus on housing because houses sold readily. This, in turn, was because individual families were able to access credit in the form of subsidized and very low interest mortgages. In short, easy credit enabled construction companies to build apartments and at the same time individuals to purchase those apartments. Obviously, this is a simplification, but the nub of the argument is valid.

In the industrial sector in Belarus, it was more difficult to obtain credit. The Soviet-era heavy industries suffered from excess staff and production compared to demand for their goods. So, increasing their indebtedness to foster production capacity made little sense. Similarly, lending to promote innovation relied on the existence of these abilities, but innovating and possessing innovative capabilities are not evident in industries that, for many years, have foregone modernization. As a result, most of the country's large industries were in no position to accrue debt in order to invest because there was no chance they would be able to repay loans, even at low interest rates. Various agricultural activities did benefit from the availability of credit, but for simplicity's sake we shall not consider this part of the economy here.

To return to the construction sector, was it not a good idea to use credit to build houses and then to grant subsidized loans for their purchase? The availability of credit supported investment in real estate and met the population's demand for housing. It allowed the creation of wealth in the form of housing stock and investment in real estate supported the Belarusian economy, which experienced high growth rates at certain times. However, the Belarusian authorities tended to over-promote credit, which created tensions and imbalances.

Easy credit enabled families to spend more than their incomes and to get into debt. Had the interest rates on their loans been less favourable, they would have had to devote more of their income to repaying the interest on the loans. Had they not decided to become indebted, they would have had to use a part of their income to pay rent. In both cases, easy credit allowed them to use more of their income for consumption other than housing. Similarly, easy credit allowed construction companies to create numerous construction sites, which, in turn, created demand for the goods needed for construction activity. Overall, this high level of demand from households and construction companies, exceeded the country's production capacity. That is, at times, households' demand for consumer goods and investment in construction could not be satisfied by domestic production.

When demand exceeds supply, the balance often is

restored through an increase in prices. However, in Belarus inflation was low because, in the best tradition of planned economies, most prices were regulated. This included the prices of many food products, utilities and transport. In short, easy credit led to excess demand, but not to high inflation. The favourable credit facilities promoted strong growth in the purchasing capacities of households and construction companies, more particularly because inflation was stable and many goods were subject to regulated prices. In turn, stable prices did not erode the purchasing capacity of households or construction companies and, therefore, did not help to contain demand and restore the balance.

The more expert reader will understand that if there is excess demand, no rise in domestic goods prices and no increase in domestic supply to satisfy that excess demand, the solution is to increase imports. Indeed, the effects of the imbalance was felt in the foreign accounts. The granting of easy credit created two problems. The first was that productive activity was concentrated in the construction industry, which is a sector that produces non-tradable goods. The second was that, as already mentioned, it allowed families to acquire their own homes at low cost and, therefore, allowed them to devote a substantial part of their income to other purchases. To be clear: guaranteeing low-price housing is a respectable policy; it becomes problematic if it becomes excessive and creates macroeconomic imbalances.

This ability to buy, based on easy credit, for years, fuelled import purchasing (especially construction materials and cars), which generated large foreign trade deficits. The excess purchasing capacity created by easy credit rather than being accompanied by a corresponding increase in domestic production, was "discharged" by purchase of imports. In a bid to maintain national pride, the political powers tried also to control the currency (Belarusian rouble) exchange rate to limit its depreciation. Thus, purchasing capacity in excess of domestic capacity to produce and an exchange rate that was too strong fuelled large trade deficits.

If countries import more than they export, they are forced to get into foreign debt to obtain the currency needed to pay for imports in excess of exports. So, a Belarusian citizen who wants to buy a German car, must pay for it in euros. If that individual is an exporter of goods to euro currency countries, this will provide them with the necessary currency; if not, the individual must borrow euros. Belarus has experienced alternating cycles of strong economic expansion thanks to easy credit, increased trade deficit and foreign debt, and phases of crisis due to foreign lenders' unwillingness to increase their credit to the country. This type of crisis occurs when a country's creditors, usually private investors, begin to doubt its ability to repay its debts. A persistent trade deficit implies that, each year, the country has to increase its debt to non-residents. At some point, after years of increasing foreign debt, it is legitimate to ask whether the country will ever be in a position to reduce it, that is, to repay (at least some of) its creditors.

To repay its foreign debt, the country has to bring its trade deficit into surplus. It must export more than it imports, so as to generate surplus in foreign currency, which can be used to repay its foreign creditors. The classic way to generate a trade surplus – and the method adopted, several times, by Belarus – is to devalue the currency (the exchange rate), to make imports more expensive for residents and exports more favourable for non-residents.

However, currency devaluation is not a painless process. In fact, a currency devaluation typically creates a significant rise in domestic prices, because the prices of imported goods increase when expressed in the devalued domestic currency. Even planned regimes do not benefit from enacting price controls on import prices: it becomes too expensive and counterproductive to subsidize imports if the aim is to reduce the trade deficit.

Some readers might not see high inflation as a major problem. However, a strong devaluation and consequent high inflation following the excesses described in Belarus, are always traumatic events. In particular, high inflation reduces (and potentially by a great deal) the purchasing power of the middle class, of employed labour, which receives a fixed wage in nominal terms, and their resulting reduction in consumption re-establishes and satisfies the budgetary constraint, as I shall explain below.

As already mentioned, devaluation makes domestic consumers poorer because the increased cost of imported goods reduces household purchasing power. In such crisis situations, inflation is created not just by more expensive imports. In many emerging economies, suppliers tend to use a strong currency (e.g. the US dollar) as their benchmark, that is, implicitly or explicitly, they set prices in that currency. If the national currency depreciates, the prices of all goods, not just imported ones, increase automatically, because traders want to keep their hard currency prices unchanged. Thus, inflation immediately follows devaluation (in technical jargon, the fraction of devaluation that passes through into prices is equal to 1). In turn, the reduction in real incomes implies a contraction in consumption and, therefore, also in imports. However, inflation is an unfair tool to use to correct imbalances, because it weighs heavily on employees, who have little control over their nominal wages. At the same time, devaluation makes domestic goods cheaper for foreign buyers, which allows exports to increase. In sum, devaluation and the related inflation allow a country to reduce its imports and increase its exports, thereby achieving a balance or a trade balance surplus. This is a necessary element to achieving a reduction in foreign debt and avoid its further increase.

In summary, in Belarus, the excesses of the era of easy credit have translated, at times, into years of crisis where devaluation and inflation have corrected imbalances and re-established the budgetary constraint (in this case, external). For some, these arguments might seem somewhat abstract. Therefore, it is useful to consider some data that confirms the phenomena described.

Leaving aside the recent movements due to the Covid-19 pandemic and the internal political crisis, over the last ten years, the Belarusian economy has suffered three balance-of-payments crises that have forced it to devalue the rouble. In January 2009 (50 per cent devaluation), in May and October 2011 (56 per cent and 42 per cent devaluation respectively) and in January 2015 (23 per cent devaluation): not a brilliant record. Between 2008 and 2018, inflation averaged more than 20 per cent. Figure 2.1 shows how the Belarusian rouble exchange rate rose from 0.2 to 2 roubles per dollar over ten years, a process that saw the value of the Belarusian currency fall by a factor of 10. After the devaluations in 2009 and 2011, inflation reached very high levels (up to 60 per cent), despite the fact that, as already seen, the prices of many goods were controlled.

Figure 2.1 Belarus: exchange rate against the US dollar (monthly data, 2005–17)

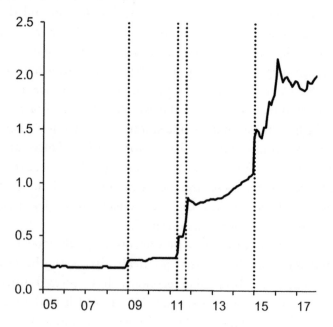

Source: IMF.

Figure 2.2 shows that the devaluations were preceded by a substantial widening of the trade deficit (the right-hand scale shows the current account balance of the balance of payments, the trade deficit being its main component), which narrowed following the devaluations. Although at the time of the 2009 devaluation, the trade deficit was 12 per cent of GDP, improving to 8 per cent in 2011 and, just over 3 per cent in 2015, this tenfold reduction in the value of the Belarusian currency did not eliminate the trade deficit.

Figure 2.2 Belarus: current account deficit (% of GDP) and GDP growth rate (annual data, 2005–17)

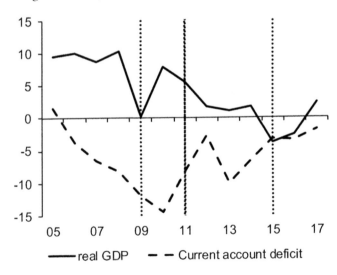

Source: IMF.

All the devaluations were accompanied by sharp falls in economic activity. Figure 2.2 depicts the sharp decline in 2009, the continued fall in 2011 and the deep recession in 2015. The decline in domestic activity, due largely to lower domestic consumption and investment, contributed to the improvements in the trade deficit in the years following the devaluations. However, the rebalancing of the external deficit was accompanied by progressively weaker domestic growth.

It should be noted that allowing inflation to correct imbalances is easy politically. The ruling party can put the blame for the crisis on foreign financial "speculators" who seek to weaken the economy and bet against the domestic currency. This avoids national politicians having to take any responsibility. There are, however, alternatives, but politically they are more costly. One can raise interest rates and, thus, reduce credit expansion (in the case of Belarus) or one can compensate the effects of easy credit by imposing restrictive policies such as reducing public spending. For the politician or head of government, this can mean backing down and reversing previous policies – in short, admitting to a mistake.

At this point, I would like to note an important difference between the example we are discussing and other countries that have been mentioned. Spain, which belongs to a monetary union (the euro), did not devalue or create domestic inflation when it was engulfed by crisis in 2011. The correction in Spain was made mainly by the containment of domestic labour costs through restrictive policies. These policies, in some respects, were more transparent than those that might have accompanied a strong currency devaluation, but, from a political point of view, certainly were costlier.

The cost of losing credibility

When a country allows its domestic credit to run too fast, leading eventually to foreign deficits, devaluations and inflation, not only do the most vulnerable pay the bill but the bill also increases.

To understand this, let us assume that the central bank has strong credibility, which means that were it to announce an inflation target, the public and investors would be confident that the target would be achieved within the given time frame. In this extreme case of the highest credibility, the central bank would achieve its inflation target simply by announcing it; the agents would immediately adjust their expectations to make them consistent with the central bank target. Suppliers and producers would raise prices in line with expected price increases. If they were to increase more, they would risk being too expensive and losing market shares. The same would apply to workers were they to demand a wage increase. In turn, the money supply would be regulated to meet everyone's expectations of the price increases in a balanced way and in line with the central bank's objective.

A high level of credibility, therefore, is particularly useful for a central bank that needs to recover from high inflation. However, more often the situation is different. If inflation rises above expectations, the central bank loses credibility just when faith in it is most needed to restore the situation. Therefore, in most cases, central banks faced with the task of stabilizing inflation after a crisis have low levels of credibility, making the stabilization process more expensive.

A central bank that has a low level of credibility might announce an inflation target, but the economic agents will not rely on it. In fact, they know that if they adjust their expectations to the central bank's objective and set low wages and do not increase prices, the central bank will likely inject more money into the economy than is consistent with the announced inflation target. This might achieve the dual objective of low inflation, since economic agents have set their prices in line with the inflation target announced, and higher economic activity supported by strong monetary expansion. Activity might grow in this scenario: monetary expansion would generate easy low-rate credit, which would stimulate demand. How many politicians would not welcome such a situation? This is described by economists as the "intertemporal inconsistency" of policies, because the policy-maker has an interest in announcing a course of action, but then also in deviating from the plan at a later point (classic contributions on this include Kydland & Prescott 1977 and Barro & Gordon 1983).

The result is that the economic agents continue to behave in anticipation of high inflation and the central bank can find it very difficult to eradicate these expectations and bring inflation to lower levels. In order to reduce inflation, the central bank must impose draconian monetary contraction policies and force the country into a recession. This will squeeze demand to such an extent that producers will be forced to contain prices, if they want to continue selling their products. The result will be continuing recession and unemployment and, before recovery, the country will have suffered high inflation, recession and unemployment.

To understand the importance of central bank credibility, consider the case of Argentina. An immediate indicator of the lack of credibility of the Central Bank of Argentina (CBA) has been the frequent changes of governor. From 1945 to 2020, it has had 60 governors with an average term of 15 months. So, were you to be offered the position of Governor of the CBA, I would advise you to think twice! This high turnover can be attributed to two reasons. First, the CBA's low credibility made the job extremely difficult; it is hard to achieve inflation and exchange rates similar to those of other more credible central banks. Second, the CBA is not independent and as soon as it does not deliver on the ruling party's plans, the reaction is to find a new governor and blame the failings on the previous one.

Argentina's recent history in this regard is enlightening (Sturzenegger & Zettelmeyer 2007). At the beginning of the 1990s, Argentina made the decision to establish a currency board with a one-to-one exchange rate with the US dollar in an attempt to stabilize inflation. A currency board is an extreme exchange rate regime, in which the central bank can print national currency (in Argentina's case, pesos) only if it acquires sufficient dollars to cover each unit of domestic currency issued. The regime is extreme because the growth in the money supply is constrained by the dollar amounts entering the country, which, as we have seen, usually stem from a balance of payments surplus. In the case of Argentina, the currency board was essential to reassure Argentinians that they could exchange their pesos for dollars at any time. Indeed, many Argentinians got so used to the one-to-one exchange rate with the dollar that many companies became indebted abroad because the interest rates on dollar loans were lower than those on peso loans.

However, this draconian measure was not enough in the long run. At the end of the 1990s, the US dollar strengthened accompanied by the Argentinian peso, based on the decision to maintain the one-to-one exchange rate. This led to a contraction in exports and contributed to a deep recession. At this point, the CBA's lack of credibility and the lack of credibility of the Argentinian economic policy authorities more generally, was re-emphasized and took on a decisive role: the expectation grew among Argentinians and the markets that the authorities would not be able to operationalize the restrictive policies necessary to support the currency board and they would decide on a currency devaluation.

This triggered a crisis of historic significance. The banks had frequently extended dollar loans to domestic companies whose revenues were in the domestic currency, leaving them unable to repay these dollar loans once the devaluation actually occurred. Bank savers began to withdraw their dollar deposits, fearing that the banks' dollar reserves might be exhausted and the banks might fail;

this triggered capital flight. In short, those able to grab dollars, even if it meant changing pesos into dollars, did so unhesitatingly. The CBA soon ran out of dollars and was forced to abandon the one-to-one exchange rate and let the currency fluctuate. The peso depreciated sharply and all the debts contracted by Argentinians, including the government, with foreigners in dollars, became impossible to repay. Hence, the 2001 Argentinian default on sovereign debt.

Figures 2.3 and 2.4 depict these events. In the late 1990s, the trade deficit began to increase, reaching values close to 5 per cent of GDP in 1998 and causing a sharp slowdown in growth (Figure 2.3). In 2001, the peso was devalued,

Figure 2.3 Argentina: current account deficit (% of GDP) and GDP growth rate (annual data, 1998–2005)

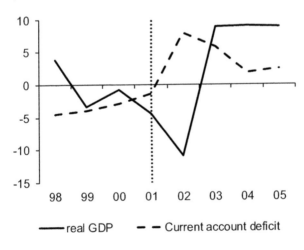

Source: IMF

causing a rapid increase in inflation (Figure 2.4). Inflation and devaluation contained domestic demand and, within a few years, the trade deficit turned into a surplus.

Figure 2.4 Argentina: exchange rate against the US dollar and inflation (annual data, 1998–2005)

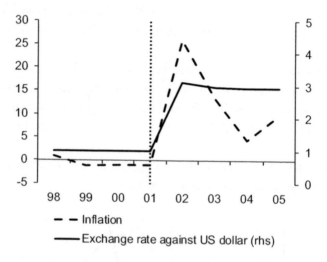

Source: IMF

To avoid an exhaustive examination of all the many and complex stages that led to the crisis, it is enough to remember that a lack of credibility had characterized economic policy management in Argentina for a very long time and was a continuing problem for the country making crises more likely (it is no coincidence that Argentina had again entered a crisis in 2018) and more expensive to correct to restore the macroeconomic stability. In other words, once lost, credibility is difficult to recover and, in the context of managing monetary policy, is fundamental. Therefore, policy-makers who stimulate the economy by excessive credit (as in the case of Belarus), not only risk facing crises that, ultimately, weigh on the middle and working classes but also lose any credibility in the management of economic policy, which makes it even more difficult to stabilize the situation after a crisis. Also, it makes any stabilization process particular costly for citizens.

The importance of credit and its limits

I do not want the reader to conclude from what has been said so far that credit is bad. On the contrary credit is at the heart of the economy and is essential to its functioning. However, it is important to know its limits.

Central banks can print new money and add it to their existing stocks if the demand for money grows. For example, demand for money would increase if prices increased, because more money would need to be in circulation to make the same purchases at these higher prices. Similarly, demand for money grows if real national production grows, because there is a need for more money to pay for the increased sales and purchases accompanying higher levels of production. Demand for money grows when the interest rate is low, as the lower the amount of interest paid on other assets, for example government bonds, the higher the investor's willingness to hold onto money. It increases also during periods of high uncertainty, as agents want to hold liquid assets as a buffer against unexpected events. These last two circumstances applied during the height of the Covid-19 pandemic.

But if the amount of new money created is higher than the increased demand for money, agents will not want to hold it and most likely will exchange it for bonds, increasing bond prices and further compressing interest rates, or for other financial assets, inflating their value. It can also happen that some excess liquidity gets spent in consumption, creating some upward price pressure.

The increased amount of currency in circulation and, therefore, the printing of new money, has been described as "seigniorage", because the state (or rather the central bank), in its function as printer of the currency, benefits from the power to print it and, therefore, could appropriate the goods that this new currency could buy (seigniorage). In reality, the central bank is part of the state and passes on to the Treasury the profits it makes, including that derived from seigniorage.

In practice, it is not so simple or easy to understand. Our ability to make payments relies not only on the value of our cash (coins and notes) but also on the availability of our bank accounts (in the form of cheques, transfers, credit cards, etc.). Here, something occurs which might seem rather magical. The central bank, in addition to printing currency notes, can credit cash on the current accounts of private banks. This credit is accomplished very simply, at a keystroke, with no requirement for the central bank to actually print anything. Then the private banks find that they have cash in their accounts at the central bank, which they can use to grant loans to customers. Thus, banks play a crucial role in the economic system, because they facilitate transformation of the liquidity created by the central bank into loans to the economy. However, note that these central bank credits are usually loans to private banks which must, in turn, provide (collateral) guarantees to the central bank in order to obtain a loan. Therefore, although it is true that central banks create money, they only lend it and do not give it away. Also, the banks that receive these loans are obliged to repay them at a certain point. We return to this later.

Private banks can use the funds lent to them by the central bank to grant loans, for example, to entrepreneurs who want to start a business and need funds. The entrepreneur who has obtained a loan then can begin a productive activity, which must generate "added value", that is, a return higher than the costs incurred to start the business. For example, suppose the entrepreneur decides to invest in growing tomatoes. They apply for a loan from the bank to rent the land, pay the workers, buy seed, pay for water, heat, etc. Ultimately, the sale of the tomatoes must earn the entrepreneur sufficient money to allow repayment of the loan with interest and, it would be hoped, to generate some profit. It should be noted that, in the absence of the bank, which is aware of the reliability of its customers, it would be difficult for the entrepreneur to begin operations based on credit from the various suppliers.

The profit that is left is the entrepreneur's income. Part of it will be consumed by the entrepreneur and part will be saved and deposited in a bank and will add to the amount of resources from which the bank can draw to make other loans. What matters is that this tomato production was made possible by the initial loan granted by the bank to the entrepreneur. The loan enabled the farmer to start tomato production activity, which led to an increase in national tomato production. This role of the banking system, to grant loans to start productive activities that increase national income, is fundamental and places banks (or the credit system, more generally) at the centre of the economic system. However, if the farmer has made a mistake in his or her planning and the revenue from the tomato sales is insufficient to repay the loan, the bank will suffer a loss. That is, it will be unable to recoup the resources lent with interest. If banks make too many bad loans, they accumulate losses and might even be forced to declare bankruptcy.

If many of a state's banks are in difficulties, this could trigger a banking crisis where the losses on the loans of various banks are so high that their assets are insufficient to repay all of their savers' deposits. Typically, this situation causes a run on the banks, which further reduces their liquidity. In such cases, the credit system is frozen and the banks may be forced to demand repayment of loans granted to their customers, potentially putting at risk entrepreneurs who have immobilized the funds received in productive investments (in our example, tomato cultivation). Thus, the virtuous loop of credit is halted and begins to reverse, with negative impacts on economic activity. The 2008 financial crisis displayed many of these characteristics; many initial losses in the banking system were linked to loans granted to purchase housing (mortgages), whose prices had decreased from the high valuations of the early 2000s (see Laeven & Valencia 2018 for a list of banking crises in the advanced countries and those that experienced a crisis in 2007–09).*

The credit mechanism is delicate: it can lead to bank failures and crises, but, I hope I have shown its importance for economic development and growth. Some clarification is needed at this point as we need to return to the issue of understanding what happens to the loan made by the central bank to the private bank, which enabled the latter to lend money to the entrepreneur. The central bank does not give money to commercial banks for free; the liquid assets the central bank credits to the accounts of private banks, in fact, are loans that require the private banks to provide collateral in the form of securities.

The private banks are obliged to repay the funds borrowed from the central bank, which are subject to interest, typically based on the interest rate set by the central bank to regulate monetary aggregates (so-called "policy rate"). If this rate is high, the banks will borrow less because it will be more difficult to find entrepreneurial projects sufficiently profitable to allow repayment at a high rate of interest. The lending bank must be able to obtain repayment of the loan from the entrepreneur to allow it to repay its loan from the central bank. If the bank fails to obtain repayment of the loan granted to the entrepreneur,

---

* For a comprehensive history of financial crises see Reinhart and Rogoff (2009).

it will record a loss, which, as already mentioned, could lead to bankruptcy. In this extreme case, the central bank will resort to the guarantee provided by the bank to avoid recording a loss in its balance sheet.

One can now appreciate why many politicians keen to grow their economies and create wealth are able to use credit to their advantage. For example, they can push their central banks to lend large amounts of money to private banks at low rates of interest, to stimulate the credit they will provide to the economy. Loans will trigger investment projects and create additional value added, which will result in more employment and higher incomes. Unfortunately, there is a limit to the amount of credit that will stimulate the economy.

Typically, in a given economy in a given time, there will be a finite number of investment projects that will show positive returns. For example, if our entrepreneur increases production, it might be that, above a certain quantity, tomatoes are difficult to sell because demand from consumers has been satisfied. This means that additional investment in tomato production is likely to be made at a loss. More generally, if the central bank over-stimulates credit, a large number of investment projects might experience a loss, that is, produce a lower return on resources (labour, seeds and land use).

All things being equal, if the value of the central bank's injection of liquidity, let us say the amount credited to the accounts of private banks, exceeds the increased production enabled by the loans made by banks to the private sector, then inflation of goods and services and/or of assets will likely result. That is, if the increase in the means of payment achieved by the granting of the loan by the private bank does not correspond to at least an equal increase in the goods produced, the effect of the loan will weigh on the economy's purchasing capacity with no corresponding increase in the supply of products.

If the monetary expansion has already led to a strong appreciation of financial assets and compressed yields, further monetary injections are likely to spill into demand for goods and services in excess of supply, resulting in upward price pressures. If the economy is open to foreign trade, this increased money supply and the corresponding demand for goods could lead to increased imports and a trade deficit. This is the ultimate constraint to which monetary policy is subject. The state cannot print money freely without some downside. However, it can print money and promote credit if this leads to increased production. Increased production becomes easier and more feasible if there is unused productive capacity in the economy. Alternatively, increased production might be triggered by improvement to the efficiency of the productive process or a reallocation of resources from lower to higher productivity activities. However, if the state prints money to excess, that is beyond what can be justified by the expected increase in production, sooner or later it will suffer crisis.

This should make what happened in Belarus in recent years clearer. The excessive growth in credit resulted in a sharp increase in the construction of real estate, but since both construction and subsequent sales of property, based on subsidized loans, relied on credit, this generated strong expansion in the purchasing capacities of both construction companies and homeowners that was greater than the ability to increase national production by a corresponding amount and, therefore, resulted in increased imports.

In short, although creating money and increasing domestic credit are two important state prerogatives, they have limits and should not be used indiscriminately unless at the cost of trade deficit, inflation, devaluations and, in some cases, bank failures. Note that inflation and devaluation are means of meeting the external budgetary constraint and bank failures can arise from violations of their budgetary constraint. So, "the potion" is not a magic one!

Central bank independence

At this point, one might wonder how the clash between economists and politicians arises. In planned-economy regimes, the political leadership controls both government and the central bank, and drives the economy centrally and without conflict. To clarify, allowing credit to run beyond its limits is not a salient feature of a planned economy; however, it has been allowed to happen often in the past. There is the example of Belarus, but also China, which has relied and continues to rely heavily on credit as an economic policy instrument. Many observers agree that credit in China has gone too far in recent years. Spain, in the years before 2008, is another good example. It is not coincidental that in many economies that we would define as advanced, the central bank is independent, that is, it manages its money and credit without explicit political interference.

However, even in the case of a more or less independent central bank, the government can succumb to the temptation to exert pressure. The classic case is where a government wants to spend in deficit (i.e. without taxing) and, in order to do so, issues government bonds (i.e. becomes more indebted). Rather than being obliged to convince domestic and foreign savers that their securities would be repaid and management of the budget would be prudent, would the politicians prefer to be able simply to sell those securities to the central bank? Is this case of central bank credit to the government any different from the credit provided to the entrepreneur who decides to produce tomatoes?

To an extent, the answer is yes. The entrepreneur increases domestic production (produces more tomatoes) and the government can invest the borrowed resources in infrastructure or improvements to the education system, for example. This would increase the country's physical and human capital and, probably, lead to increased production. However, government generally is not entrepreneurial and has different objectives. It is more likely to invest the money in consolidating its electoral support, without increasing domestic production. For example, it could increase public-sector pensions or salaries without demanding more effort from government employees, in effect, getting into debt to "give away" resources to pensioners or civil servants. In this case, domestic production may not increase and, therefore, the greater purchasing power of citizens might generate more inflation and increase imports, resulting in a trade deficit.

Here, another clarification is necessary. John Maynard Keynes (1936) taught us that if the economy is not in full employment and there is not full utilization of production potential, even "donated" money can increase national production because it activates additional demand. However, giving away money is certainly not the most efficient way to support the economy, and Keynes did not back this approach. Moreover, whether or not the economy is close to full employment is not something that politicians usually take into account, more often preoccupied by the need to win the approval of voters. In fact, there are many cases of politicians who initiate fiscal stimuli when the economy is close to full employment. President Trump, for example, introduced a strong fiscal stimulus at the beginning of 2018 when the US economy was close to its full potential. I shall return to this in the next chapter.

For these reasons, economists argue about the importance of central bank independence and, for the same reasons, politicians tend not to fully accept the idea. Think of the debate in recent years regarding the role of the European Central Bank and the fact that it should have boosted quantitative easing (QE), (i.e. the plan to buy government bonds in order to keep long-term interest rates low and, thus, stimulate investment and consumption) as well as Trump's criticism (and decision not to renew) the former chairman of the Federal Reserve Board, Janet Yellen. He also expressed his negative opinion of the Federal Reserve's interest rate management and in November 2018, further stated that he was "not even a little bit happy" that he had chosen Jerome Powell as its president. And such tensions preceded the pandemic. During the height of the Covid-19 crisis, central banks loosened monetary conditions so much and intervened in the markets buying so many government bonds that for a time politicians and economists found themselves in the same camp. But this is unlikely to last.

All in all, the consensus that the central bank should be independent is well established in advanced economies, although we should probably expect the idea to be increasingly challenged. Where the consensus is less clear and the battle rages more openly is on fiscal policy, which I discuss in the next chapter.

3

The multiplication of loaves and fishes

Senhor, your job is unenviable because you seem to have so much responsibility but have so little power. Inevitably, either you or one of your successors will soon have to take some unpleasant fiscal measures. These unpleasantries can be delayed for a time, but only by accepting increasingly large costs in terms of the severity of the adjustments that ultimately will have to be made. Your job is so difficult now because your predecessors chose to delay.

T. J. Sargent, "An open letter to the Brazilian finance minister", *Wall Street Journal*, 30 January 1986.

Fiscal policy is the other major economic instrument available to government to manage public expenditure and taxes. Clearly, fiscal policy has many aims and, here, we can only gloss over their complexities. According to Richard Musgrave's classic definition (Musgrave 1959), fiscal policy has three main functions: (1) the production of public goods; (2) the redistribution of these goods; and (3) macroeconomic stabilization. Here, we shall chiefly consider support for household income and stabilization of economic activity, that is, macroeconomic stimuli of the economy, which occur not just in times of recession, but more frequently whenever required by political imperatives, which of course includes pre-election periods.

Politicians, for electoral purposes or to maintain the consensus in favour of the current government, frequently offer aid and subsidies to their citizens. Once disbursed, it is difficult to eliminate these transfers. As time passes, their recipients become used to them and their withdrawal would likely result in huge disappointment and resentment. So, aid that is designed originally to be temporary during difficult periods, can often become permanent. A partial testament to that is how difficult it is in many countries to remove some of the fiscal programmes initiated to support the economy hit by the Covid-19 pandemic. An additional complication is that, often, such aid is financed by a deficit in order not to increase the tax burden (which, also, would result in a discontented citizenry); thus, it is not uncommon for the state to find itself with a budget that is chronically in shortfall.

The paternalistic state

Many governments and states around the world adopt a paternalistic approach – typical both of authoritarian regimes, but also, of the governments of some very advanced countries in northern Europe. A paternalistic approach means that the state provides for its citizens "from cradle to grave", which includes public education, a public health system, more or less guaranteed employment and a state pension. Some northern European countries with extremely cohesive and culturally homogeneous societies manage to achieve excellent economic performance from this policy (Alesina & Glaeser 2004). In some others, whose societies are more culturally divided in religious or ethnic terms, a paternalistic regime can be an attempt to maintain social peace.

It is clear that the weaker the regime politically, perhaps precisely because the country is divided, the greater the need for that paternalism to guarantee excessive public spending to keep most of its citizens satisfied. There are many world countries that fit broadly with this description. I have chosen one example, but, as in Chapter 2, the specific country is not strictly relevant. Also, in trying to remain faithful to the correctness of the underlying point while, at the same time, being clear and comprehensible, I have reduced the complexity of the case.

Egypt is a country with a chronic budget deficit that arises from a tradition of the Egyptian state providing a range of free services or, otherwise, supporting its citizens with basic needs. Prices of energy products (petrol, gas for cooking and heating, etc.) are kept low because they are subsidized by the state. Many food products, for example bread, are also heavily subsidized and cost very little. Similarly, at one time, there was a rule that all graduates were guaranteed a job in public administration. Although this no longer applies, the fact that such a rule once existed, explains the over-abundance of civil servants in Egypt and offers some understanding of the country's culture.

These state expenses, in part, serve to maintain calm within a highly divided and frustrated population. Egypt's recent history provides evidence of the difficulties involved in achieving this. The 2011 revolution that sought to bring down Hosni Mubarak's authoritarian regime, part of the Arab Spring uprisings, led to the election in 2012 of Mohamed Morsi, a member of the Muslim Brotherhood Sunni Muslim group. Morsi remained in power for only a year before being deposed by a military coup. Thus, in the space of three years, Egypt had three different presidents, and experienced two revolutions and a coup d'état. It is clear that, in a country so divided, the government – even when, as now, it is managed by the military – will be weak. To survive, a weak government must spend.

This explains Egypt's double-digit budget deficits in recent years and prompts the question: what are the implications of not respecting the state's budget constraints? A public expenditure deficit that is used to subsidize citizens' energy and food consumption and provide salaries for the large number of civil servants has fuelled domestic demand. As in the case of excessive credit, discussed in Chapter 2, this fiscal policy conduct has led to high levels of consumption that have far exceeded the country's production capacity. When domestic demand exceeds domestic production, in a country not willing to adjust domestic prices and cool demand accordingly (because even in Egypt many prices are controlled), large trade-balance deficits are inevitable. This is described by economists as "twin deficits", which, in Egypt's case, can be clearly seen in the data (see Figure 3.1).

Figure 3.1 Egypt: current account deficit (% of GDP) and budget deficit (% of GDP) (annual data, 2005–18)

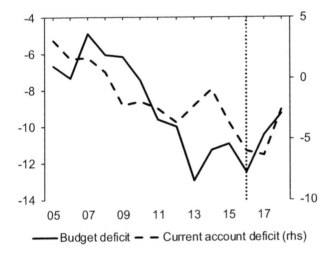

Source: IMF.

At the same time, at least until the end of 2016, Egypt tried to maintain an exchange rate pegged to the dollar. However, to sustain the exchange rate in a situation of a trade balance deficit and, therefore, with a continuous outflow of US dollars, Egypt's central bank was obliged to meet the demand for dollars. It had to sell dollars and buy Egyptian pounds continually at the fixed exchange rate. Dollars which were bought by Egyptian importers to buy goods from abroad in order to meet the additional demand caused by the growing fiscal deficit, thus closed the circle initiated by public expenditure in deficit. Indeed, the latter pushed up consumption and imports, and in turn increased the need for dollars to meet those imports and led importers to sell local currency in exchange for dollars, thus generating pressures for a currency devaluation.

At the end of 2016, the central bank's reserves (of dollars) were exhausted and it was forced to stop intervening in the foreign exchange market to support the Egyptian pound, and to let the exchange rate depreciate. The depreciation was an immediate drop (from about EGP8 to EGP18 per USD) and caused inflation to increase to 25 per cent at the beginning of 2017 (see Figure 3.2).

At this point, it is worth noting that in the examples of both Belarus (strong credit expansion) and Egypt (strong fiscal expansion in deficit), the result was a balance of payments crisis and a devaluation of the exchange rate and high domestic inflation. This is no coincidence: in both cases the stimulus applied to these economies was unsustainable. Both credit in Belarus and the budget deficit in Egypt created more demand than national production capacity could meet. This was, in part, because these countries' production capacities were structurally low and lacked the reforms to increase productivity.

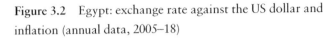

Figure 3.2 Egypt: exchange rate against the US dollar and inflation (annual data, 2005–18)

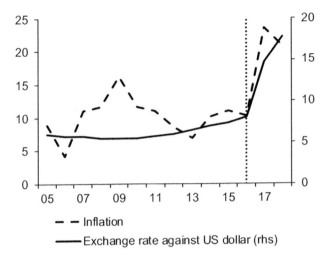

Source: IMF.

This excess demand, therefore, passed to foreign production, namely its imports. However, in order to import goods from abroad foreign currency is required (many goods in the international market, including oil, need to be paid for in US dollars). Therefore, the citizens of these countries continued to change their domestic currency into dollars, at the exchange rate guaranteed by the central bank, in order to buy imported goods. These exchange rates that were kept overvalued by the national authorities, remained in force for several years, based on the same reasoning that maintained expansive fiscal and monetary policies. Thus, the domestic cost of imported basic necessities, such as energy goods and medicines, was kept low, even though this was unsustainable in the long run. All of these measures were designed to keep the purchasing power of citizens and domestic consumption at a high level without having to pay the bill. However, budget constraints cannot be ignored forever; someone has to pay. Why is this the case?

The demand for foreign currency generated two outcomes. First, the foreign exchange reserves available at the respective central banks were exhausted. Second, the governments of these countries were obliged to borrow foreign currency from abroad to replenish their domestic currency reserves. Part of this debt increase was facilitated by politics: Belarus benefited from loans in various forms, sometimes in the form of discounts on gas and oil imports, from Russia, whereas in Egypt the Gulf Cooperation Council (GCC) provided funding to the Cairo government on several occasions. In both cases, over time, the shortage of dollars due to the large trade deficits and the unwillingness of political allies to continue financing what had become an unsustainable situation, led to crises manifested in large exchange rate devaluations.

The dynamics of these crises are simple. As long as credit or fiscal policy is excessively expansionary, citizens can consume more than they produce. This is facilitated by foreign borrowing, which allows these citizens to acquire those imports that fill the gap between demand for goods and services (high) and domestic supply (limited). However, at a certain point this situation becomes unsustainable; investors and foreign governments are no longer willing to grant further loans, which precipitates two responses: (1) repaying the debts incurred, and (2) not taking on any new debt. The latter translates into reducing the trade deficit, by returning domestic demand back to the level of domestic production. This can be achieved by reducing credit or public spending, for instance, but either way implies a retreat from the previous policies. It can be very difficult, politically, to have to admit to the electorate that it is necessary to suspend subsidies and guaranteed public employment because the money has run out. It is admission of a political failure from which few governments would be likely to recover. Moreover, if debt repayments are involved, it may be necessary to go into a trade surplus with foreign countries, which will require achieving an excess of domestic production over consumption, to enable their repayment. In this case, not only must subsidies be removed (and civil servants dismissed), but taxes must be increased. In short, all consumption that exceeded domestic production must be repaid – and with interest. This is when the budgetary constraint re-emerges.

However, more often than not, the political cost of this correction will be too high. Few governments would be willing to tell voters that pensions are too high, that there are too many public-sector workers and that subsidies have to end. Further, even if there were an intention to make a fiscal adjustment, it might be difficult to agree on the distribution of the costs among the various social classes, resulting in postponement of the stabilization (Alesina & Drazen 1991). Finally, in many cases, the time frame may be too tight to achieve an orderly adjustment in the public accounts. For instance, if foreign creditors are no longer willing to increase their financing, restoration of the external trade balance has to be immediate. This implies an instant reduction in domestic consumption, including public expenditure.

An alternative way of adjusting and meeting the budgetary constraint is to let the exchange rate of the domestic currency devalue so that imports suddenly become too expensive in the domestic market, and concurrently domestic goods become cheaper for non-residents thereby increasing exports. However, as we have seen, devaluation creates inflation, often even massive inflation, because imported goods become very expensive. Usually, devaluation is accompanied by a recession because interest rates rise (the central bank tries to contain the increase in domestic inflation by tightening its monetary policy). Thus, inflation and recession force the correction, which is what generally happens. The real incomes of citizens fall, devalued by inflation and cut by unemployment, driving down consumption and fuelling a recession. The cost of all this – if produced by a devaluation – is paid for mainly by the employed and the most vulnerable groups in the population.

Obviously, this happens because, at a certain point, the country can no longer continue to increase its external debt. In some cases, where foreign creditors are not only unwilling to increase their loans but also want their loans repaid, the situation can become unsustainable. This happens because, regardless of how much the country devalues and corrects the imbalance between consumption and domestic production, it can never create a trade surplus quickly enough to allow it to repay its debts. This is how states arrive at a crisis situation that can lead to defaults on foreign debt. Emblematic cases include Argentina in 2001 and Greece in 2012 (but these are only two in a very long list; see Laeven & Valencia 2018). In these episodes, the costs were paid by resident citizens and, also, partly by foreign savers who held these countries' debt securities. Those who had purchased Argentinian or Greek government bonds are only too well aware of this. We address the issue of defaults later; here, I simply want to make it clear that there is no "free lunch" in relation to excessively expansive monetary or fiscal policies.

Does public spending pay for itself?

In recent years, particularly following the 2008–09 financial crisis, the debate over the role of fiscal policy has become even more heated. In 2009, the major advanced countries agreed to implement a coordinated fiscal stimulus of around 2 per cent of GDP.* In the subsequent years, given the strong growth in debt-to-GDP ratios – mainly due to the recession that had reduced economic activity as well as tax revenues by opening significant budget deficits – the main advanced countries changed course and

---

* See the G20 London Summit Leaders' Statement of 2 April 2009, https://www.mofa.go.jp/policy/economy/g20_summit/2009-1/communique.pdf.

proceeded to implement measures to reduce deficits and stabilize their public debt. So-called "austerity" policies became a hugely debated issue, because some of these fiscal corrections were applied to economies that were still fragile and, rather than helping the recovery, slowed it (Pisani-Ferry 2012). This debate has taken a new turn with the Covid-19 crisis. Given the depth of the recession and the limits inherent in monetary policy to ease it further, economists and politicians have come together to call for and implement massive fiscal relief measures. Although this stance is appropriate as a countercyclical measure, it is less clear what its impact will be on the sustainability of public debt a few years down the road.

The idea I want to tackle next is that an expansive fiscal policy will generally pay for itself. That is the idea that under normal conditions, the deficit boosts the economy and generates an increase in activity and tax revenues, such that the initial increase in expenditure or reduction in revenues pays for itself and is able to avoid creation of a deficit (and, therefore, more debt). With particular reference to tax cuts, this idea was popularized by the American economist Arthur Laffer in the 1970s and has been supported by numerous politicians ever after. For example, Ronald Reagan's fiscal strategy (Auerbach & Slemrod 1997) and, more recently, that of President Trump in support of the fiscal stimulus approved at the turn of 2017 followed this idea. Typically, it re-emerges when politicians want to increase public spending or reduce taxes without having to find the corresponding finance (i.e., the means to finance these policies). This is because cutting spending to reduce taxes or increasing taxes to increase spending, is generally difficult and expensive politically.

The "deficit expenditure that pays for itself" is, in some ways, the modern attempt to repeat the miracle of the loaves and fishes, or the notion that something can be created out of nothing. Governments claim to distribute resources (e.g. to citizens in the form of increased transfers); since it lacks these resources, it has to borrow and therefore gives the beneficiaries the opportunity to increase their consumption without the need for anyone to pay higher taxes, either today or in the future. In what follows, we will see if this is possible.

Suppose that government increases spending to pay civil servants to dig and fill holes in the streets (the classic Keynesian example). It is true that this will increase the workers' incomes and, therefore, their consumption and in turn production as long as the economy is not in a situation of full employment and full use of resources. However, this does not mean that economic activity will increase enough to repay the initial budgetary expenditure.

Take a simple numerical example: the government hires a hundred public workers to dig and fill holes in the ground and pays them £1 each. Since these workers are on a low income (£1), we can assume that they will consume all of this income to feed themselves. Therefore, the purchase of food and the production of food increase by £100. This increased food purchase corresponds to an additional £100 of income for the farmers, who produced the ingredients, and the workers in the production chain involved in producing the additional food. Let us assume, now, that the state finances itself with a 50 per cent tax on all citizen incomes. The additional £100 of production (and, therefore, the incomes of all those who have contributed to producing the additional food) will provide the state with an additional £50 of tax revenue. So, £100 more expenditure and £50 more revenue results in a deficit of £50.

Under what conditions would the additional expenditure finance itself? What would lead to an increase in revenue equivalent to £100? In the example above, this will happen if public expenditure produces at least twice the output, that is, if the public expenditure "multiplier" – that is the increase in GDP for a given increase in public spending – is at least 2. This is conditional on the assumption in the example that the state taxes income at a rate of 50 per cent, which is quite high. In this case, the £100 spent will translate into £200 more in production and £100 more in revenue. Why does the additional £100 spending on food lead to an increase in total demand of £200? Again, Keynes teaches us that there is a demand multiplier linked to the fact that the extra initial additional demand (the £100) creates additional income (£100 in the example), which, in turn, creates additional demand. However, expenses with a multiplier of at least 2 are infrequent in normal times (Batini *et al.* 2014). Certainly, in crisis situations, when, perhaps, monetary policy has limited effectiveness because it has already brought interest rates to zero, fiscal policy can be more effective. There are many academic contributions that show how this could happen (e.g. Auerbach & Gorodnichenko 2012). Indeed, this helps explain the unanimous support for the large fiscal expansion enacted by many countries to counteract the effects of the pandemic. Still, under more normal conditions it is more difficult, if not impossible, to increase spending without growing the fiscal deficit.

Get into debt to invest

Some politicians have argued that if deficit spending is concentrated in highly productive investments, not only will the deficit not increase but also the ratio of public debt to output may reduce. Again, I offer an example. Let us suppose that every dollar spent on public investments generates two dollars of output (i.e. investments have a multiplier of 2, again quite high). This means that, not only does investment spending lead to quite a large increase in demand but also that the infrastructure thus produced increases the efficiency of the productive system as a whole and enables private production to be greater than the increase in demand triggered by the public investment. Let us suppose that government increases investment spending by 1 percentage point of GDP in a given year and keeps it at the new higher level from then onwards. Given the multiplier of 2, GDP would grow by 2 per cent more than it would have if investment had not increased in the first year, and then would remain stable at the new level in subsequent years, if public investment does not increase further. In this scenario, what happens to the deficit and the debt?

Expenditure is 1 percentage point of GDP higher each year, which is equal to the additional investment. Assuming, as above, that revenues are 50 per cent of GDP, as GDP increases by 2 percentage points, revenues increase by 1 percentage point of GDP, so no further deficit is created. Assuming, for simplicity, an original balanced budget, the debt ratio will actually fall because the deficit remains unchanged, but GDP grows.

Should we conclude that the idea works? It does, but it is important to keep in mind what happens in a few years' time. In this example, investment spending increased by 1 percentage point of GDP per year. Therefore, every year we spend more than previously on investments (e.g. on infrastructure). At some point, it must be assumed that the very high return (good) investment opportunities available to government will dry up. After investing 1 additional percentage point of GDP for several years, it is reasonable to assume that the most productive opportunities will have been exhausted. Suppose that, at that point, government stops making the additional investment of 1 percentage point of GDP. Then what happens is that investment expenditure is reduced by 1 percentage point of GDP compared to the previous year, which reduces GDP – and substantially, given the high multiplier.

Nevertheless, I want to stress the following. If public expenditure is highly productive, in the example public investment increases income two-fold, then it might be the case that the increase in expenditure pays for itself and that it does not increase the deficit. This is the position taken recently, for example by the IMF, in support of large public investment programmes as a way to support economies out of the pandemic recession (IMF 2020). However, we must exercise caution, as in normal times multipliers of 2 or more are rarely found and are especially rare if the country is highly indebted. This is because the additional expenditure could lead to a further increase in indebtedness, if later it turns out that the investments made were less productive than expected. And history has plenty of examples of investment pushes by the public sector that were less successful than were hoped for, essentially because they cost more money and were less productive than planned. This uncertainty over the outcome of the public investment programme could lead to increases in the risk premium required by investors to hold government bonds and, therefore, in interest rates, which would probably offset the positive impact of the increased spending.*

Public investments with high returns do exist but are often not at the top of the politicians' lists. For example, consider investment in education, research, environmental sustainability and infrastructure maintenance. These types of investment accumulate over time, in the sense that they create a growing stock of capital. In the case of education,

---

* The example assumes that the budget would be balanced before the increase in investment spending. Had we started with a deficit, the increased investment in our example would not have created an additional deficit nor would it have eliminated the previous deficit. The debt would have been on an increasing trajectory before the increase in investment, and this increase would have partly offset its decline due to the high-yield investments we assumed.

better training of primary school children means that, after five years, five cohorts of children in middle school and high school will be better trained, and after ten years, ten cohorts will be better trained, and so on. Over time the effects of these expenses are not depleted, but persist and contribute to increasing the country's human capital. Similarly, with research, discoveries and knowledge tend to accumulate over time. As does the effect of public investment in the context of environmental sustainability. Consider expenditure to secure watercourses, to build houses in areas less at risk from natural disasters, to monitor natural phenomena, these expenditures accumulate rendering the country's productive and housing capital safer and more resilient to climate effects over time. The benefits of such expenditure in the medium to long term can be extremely high.

Therein lies the problem – that these types of expenditure require a medium to long-term horizon, not only in relation to their planning and implementation but also in relation to appreciation of their benefits. For example, investing in education does not bring immediate benefits in terms of growth and material well-being. Voters, who, among other things, are no longer in receipt of education, may value this type of expenditure less or feel that it does not provide them with any benefit. Thus, these expenses may not be at the top of the politicians' agendas. It is not surprising that debate often focuses on increasing transfers (pensions, subsidies) and reducing taxes. Rarely a politician's main campaign message is a promise to spend more on primary schools, or reduce hydro-geological instability, or invest in research. Paradoxically, even if the politician tries to promote such issues, there is a tendency that various lobbies will try to exploit these good intentions; for example, a school reform can become an opportunity to hire large numbers of teachers.

In short, only in extreme cases does the public spending that politicians favour (typically, transfers and lower taxes) "pay for itself". Economists will continue to argue that their studies find high multipliers only in acute situations, for example, if the economy is suffering severe recession and monetary policy has brought rates to a minimum. However, in most other situations it is very difficult to have such high multipliers although, for most politicians, expenditure multipliers will always be high, especially in the short term, and particularly in the run-up to an election or immediately afterwards when an electoral promise needs fulfilling.

4

Something for nothing?

"There's no such thing as a free lunch"
                              Milton Friedman, 1975.

In the previous chapters I have shown that budgetary constraints should always be respected. When economists refer to there being no such thing as a free lunch, they mean that everything comes at a cost, and nothing is created from nothing. From time to time, most of us do get a free lunch as the result of an invitation from someone not looking for anything in return. However, in economics – and macroeconomics, in particular – nothing is free, which says much about the science of economics and the economists who add up the numbers and assess the budgetary compatibilities. In contrast, for politicians the temptation to make someone else pay for their possible excesses is strong. In the case of the macroeconomic policies discussed in this book, this temptation can take the form of reluctance to repay debts taken on by the state, especially, if they are high.

Making others pay

When, in 2001, Argentina defaulted on its foreign public debt, the domestic situation had become unsustainable (Sturzenegger & Zettelmeyer 2007). We have already mentioned that, towards the end of the 1990s, Argentina entered a recession. During that time, the authorities increased both public spending and the budget deficit while maintaining a fixed one-to-one exchange rate with the US dollar. We have seen the results of this combination of excessive public spending and overvalued exchange rates in the case of Egypt and, similarly, the Argentinians were quick to begin shopping abroad and increasing their trade deficit. Among other reasons, the government could not get into debt in the domestic currency (peso) because no one trusted the currency or was willing to buy securities in pesos. Investors and savers feared that, sooner or later, the government would be forced into an exchange rate devaluation, which would result in domestic inflation based on the country's past history and the credibility of its politicians and institutions. Thus, most of Argentina's debt was issued in dollars with foreign creditors. This resulted in a volatile situation and an eventual decision by foreign investors to stop financing Argentina any further.

Argentina was unable to renew the dollar bonds that were expiring and was obliged to repay them. The availability of dollars at the central bank was limited and soon it was unable to repay the maturing securities. So, what could the authorities do? The options were limited, consisting essentially of an exchange rate devaluation to correct the trade deficit, and defaulting on the foreign debt because of the central bank's inability to repay it.

Defaulting on foreign debt translates into a loss for non-resident investors holding securities that are not repaid. From the politician's viewpoint, it might seem (cynically speaking) an effective way to reduce the state's public debt at the lowest possible cost. If the holders of public securities are residents of some other country then they will pay the bill. Not a bad solution, the politician might think, because these citizens of other states are not part of their electorate. However, in reality, although the foreign holders of Argentinian bonds paid part of the bill, Argentina's residents also faced high costs.

Under the uncompromising laws of economics, budgetary constraints must be acknowledged. As in the case of the other crises we have examined, Argentina's led to devaluation, inflation and recession, conditions that were necessary to correct the trade deficit. The reduction in labour income and the erosion of household purchasing power resulting from the inflation and unemployment, as in the other examples presented in this book, represented a dire cost for the population.

However, Argentinians also faced other costs. Many had bank savings accounts, which they tried to protect during the crisis by converting these savings into dollars or taking them abroad (capital flight). This drained liquidity from Argentina's local banks and resulted in the government blocking current accounts and closing down some banks. For around 12 months, most Argentinians did not have full access to their bank accounts. When they regained access, they found that their savings in pesos had lost about two-thirds of their value as a result of the devaluation and inflation. Both their income and savings were reduced.

Does making others pay work?

Charging others is one option that politicians may try to pursue. The idea is simple: I have spent more than I should have done and have got myself into debt. So, now I should reduce my consumption below current levels and not increase my savings but use the money to repay my debt. Or should I? Why not repudiate the debt instead?

First, we need to be clear about what "repudiating the debt" means. A state can default on its debt, that is stop paying interest and principal, or it can restructure its debt, that is offer a more or less coercive exchange of new bonds for the old ones. New bonds typically have longer maturities and pay lower interest rates, in this way provide a reduction of the debt burden. Argentina in 2001 defaulted on its debt and then started a restructuring process in 2005.

If the debtors of the state are predominantly resident citizens, then defaulting on the public debt results in the sudden imposition of a high tax on citizens' savings, a policy which inevitably provokes strong resistance. However, even if the debt holders are mostly foreign citizens, this does not imply there is no cost. After it defaulted in 2001,

Argentina for various reasons was unable to issue debt in the international capital market for almost ten years. Confidence in the country had evaporated (who would want to buy government bonds from a country that had just reneged on its debt?). Even after 2005, some of the debt restructuring had left a substantial legal legacy preventing Argentina from issuing new debt in the international market. Many holders of Argentine bonds that had not been fully repaid had taken legal action and, in some cases, achieved a ruling that, if Argentina were to issue bonds in the international market, the funds raised would initially be used to repay these bond holders (*Financial Times*, 22 April 2016). Thus, it was pointless for the Argentinian government to issue new debt in the international market if the proceeds were destined to repay old debts. In other words, repaying the creditors it had defaulted on in 2001 with the proceeds of new debts would constitute an abdication from the earlier decision not to repay.

Inability to access the international capital market imposes serious constraints. Essentially, it means that the country can only import goods and services to the value of what it can export. It must maintain the current account of the balance of payments in balance or in surplus. For countries such as Argentina, which export mainly food products, this implies volatility in export earnings and, therefore, a lack of ability to rely on a stable flow of imports, perhaps to meet energy needs and to allow long-term investment. In fact, in Argentina's case, in the years following the 2001 default, the world price of food items produced and exported by Argentina grew substantially, meaning it was not so costly for the country not to be able to borrow abroad.

In summary, defaulting on foreign debt is an extreme way of satisfying the budget constraint; rather than being repaid, the debts are written off. Although it might seem a somewhat attractive solution, it does not eliminate all the costs entailed by past excesses. The trade deficit that led to the accumulation of external debt needs to be corrected. If restrictive (monetary and fiscal) policies, which are politically expensive, cannot achieve this, then an economic crisis is required to make the correction. The associated devaluation, inflation, recession, unemployment and reduced incomes and savings, in addition to the legal battles with creditors trying to recover their investments, which could drag on for many years, are extremely damaging politically. Finally, the loss of credibility in relation to the management of economic policies cannot be underestimated and, inevitably, makes macroeconomic adjustments even costlier, as shown by Argentina's efforts to contain inflation following the 2001 crisis (see Chapter 2).

Central banks to the rescue

Another misconception that is becoming increasingly popular among politicians is the idea that central banks can simply keep printing money to allow them to buy unlimited amounts of government bonds. In other words, that central banks can unproblematically swallow unlimited amounts of excess public spending, in which case, all we need do is convince, or force, central bankers to act accordingly.

We discussed the limits of monetary policy in Chapters 1 and 2. However, here we are addressing a somewhat different question. When the central bank buys government bonds, their seller is paid with newly printed money, which increases the amount of money held by the private sector. To a certain extent, central bank purchase of government bonds can be achieved without increasing this amount, that is, without any "easing" of the monetary conditions. This can be achieved in various ways. For instance, a central bank might first sell off some holdings on the asset side of its balance sheet to make room for government bonds; however, the amounts of these other assets tend to be limited and can include mainly foreign reserves and gold, which does not allow much scope to increase the bank's government bond holdings. In addition, selling its reserves depletes the central bank of an important asset and will have effects on the exchange rate, typically leading to an appreciation which may be unwelcome.

Another possibility would be to buy more government bonds and then try to absorb this additional liquidity by increasing the interest rate paid on banks' deposits at the central bank, which would provide an incentive to maintain these deposits with the central bank and not lend their liquidity to the economy. However, this possibility could turn out to be very costly for the central bank and is, therefore, not popular. If the return on the asset side of the central bank balance sheet is lower than the interest paid on banks' deposits, the central bank will run losses and its capital will be depleted. This situation could be maintained for a time without causing a major problem, but could not go on forever. Also, the banks will have a great deal of their liquidity in their current accounts with the central bank, which they can access at any time. This makes the system unstable. Argentina provides a good example of the limits of this strategy. Although the amounts in deposit accounts of commercial banks with the central bank may be receiving a reasonable rate of interest, they are still liquid and can be accessed very quickly. In Argentina, in the run up to the 2018 crisis, the holders of central bank liquidity started to change it for dollars, leading to the exchange rate collapse.

The more conventional approach, and the one pursued during the Covid-19 crisis by most central banks, is to buy government bonds to increase the liquidity in the system. I pointed out in Chapter 2 that there are drawbacks to having excess liquidity. Although it may not lead to substantial consumer inflation, it definitely leads to a rise in asset and property prices and exacerbates the current account deficit. In addition, it acts as an incentive for the private and public sectors to borrow. These situations can't go on forever. So, the question is how many government bonds can the central bank absorb without it jeopardizing its macroeconomic stability objective? Is this amount finite or potentially infinite?

The answer is that it is most definitely finite. Indeed, once the government incurs an unsustainable fiscal position, the central bank can be forced to print endlessly to buy government bonds. By this point in the book, the reader should have an understanding of the importance of central bank independence for the ability to control inflation, and the impact of excess liquidity on consumer and asset inflation and on the current account.

Although the central bank's amount of bond holding may be finite, it can be quite sizeable. Take the frequently cited example of Japan, whose central bank (the Bank of Japan, BoJ) currently holds almost 100 per cent of GDP in government bonds. This is undoubtedly helpful for the Japanese government for one main reason. The BoJ's seigniorage, or privilege to print money, allows it to print money to purchase government bonds. And, since the BoJ is a public entity, its seigniorage acts as a source of financing for the government. The government exploits this privilege by selling its bonds to the BoJ and spending the money received in exchange for them. The bonds remain on the BoJ balance sheet and the BoJ returns to the Japanese Treasury the interest received on these bonds because central banks pay their profits to the government. They are public entities so, bearing in mind that seigniorage is the amount of new money printed by the central bank, the higher the seigniorage, the more advantageous for the government. Since the seigniorage is the amount of new money printed by the central bank, it defines the central bank's monetary stance.

However, the large purchase of government bonds carries a risk that the government becomes overstretched and gradually – or in some cases very rapidly – slips into an unsustainable fiscal position. That is, it reaches a level of debt that, under reasonable assumptions, it will be unable to repay in the future. So, what are the consequences? One obvious consequence is that the central bank could suffer a loss in the value of some of its assets, specifically the government bonds, and – if these losses are sufficiently large – its capital will be wiped out. In this case, it would be left with more liabilities than assets, but still able to print money. Nowadays, money is fiat money. Its value is based not on some real asset, such as gold, but on the fact that it is the legal tender that can be used for payments, including tax payments. So, unless one is concerned about inflation and the value of money, there is no reason for not wanting to hold it even if the central bank has negative capital. In other words, one should hold onto one's money for as long as there are no expectations of inflation or devaluation that would reduce its real value.

This then raises the problem that the central bank's reduced assets might limit its ability to control inflation. If or when it needs to reduce the liquidity in the system, this might require it to sell some assets in exchange for money. If there are insufficient assets on its balance sheet, the central bank might be unable to guarantee full control of inflation. If it tries to reduce the liquidity by increasing the interest rate paid on reserves (banks' deposits at the central bank), it will likely be forced to run a loss since the returns on the asset side of the balance sheet may fall short of the interest paid on the liability side. These losses will reduce its capital even further and the central bank will not be able to raise finance by printing money because this would contravene its goal of reducing the amount of money in the system. Therefore, the only solution is to sell some assets, but the amount of these is limited and finite, therefore sooner or later the situation will become unsustainable. In this case, it is likely that the central bank will let monetary conditions run loose and choose not to mop up the extra liquidity, in the hope that the monetary stimulus could bring about higher inflation and an increase in the demand for money and, therefore, profits, thereby reinstating its capital.

Before proceeding further, I would like to address an issue that might be of interest to some readers. There is little difference between the government selling government bonds to the central bank and using the receipts to finance public spending and then defaulting on the bonds and the central bank printing money and giving it directly to citizens. It is clear that the second option – known as "helicopter money" – is not fundamentally different to the first option. Both involve increasing the money supply without it being backed by an increase in central bank assets and, therefore, reducing central bank capital or rendering it negative. We have just discussed the implications of this option in terms of reducing the ability of central banks to credibly fight inflation, if the need arises. However, "helicopter money" implies that the central bank should pick and choose whom to transfer the money to and how much, a role which is better left to fiscal policy and to the politically nominated officials who run it. It is not the role of the central bank to decide over how to distribute government revenues to the public. Therefore, we would expect central banks to avoid this route.

In summary, central banks certainly can hold sizeable amounts of government bonds; there are advanced economy examples such as Japan. However, although sizeable, the amount must be finite. As central banks go down the path of continuously increasing their holdings of government bonds – as happened after the 2008 financial crisis and even more decisively during the Covid-19 crisis – it is important that they retain their independence and keep their potential losses in check. Central banks are – quite rightly – coming to the rescue, but they will have to strike the fine balance between maintaining stability and falling into crisis.

What does China teach us?

The case of the People's Republic of China is certainly both relevant and remarkable for our discussion. China relies heavily on monetary and fiscal policies to stimulate its economy but has yet to face an economic crisis. Even the Covid-19 recession in the first quarter of 2020 was short-lived. Notwithstanding that China is a highly developed, centrally controlled economy, and a very complex case, it too cannot escape budget constraints.

China is run by a single-party political system and lacks the typical electoral cycle of democracies. Elections in China are markedly different. The system is strictly controlled by the Communist Party, which is never challenged by direct electoral competition. Nevertheless, the Chinese and other similar regimes maintain their legitimacy by ensuring constant improvements to the living conditions of their citizens.

The Chinese Communist Party, in the best socialist tradition, formulates five-year plans that set targets for economic growth. In recent years, these five-year plans have become less specific, not least because the Party no longer has control over a large part of the economy. The American Peterson Institute for International Economics estimates that the private sector share of Chinese productive economic activity is now around three-quarters; however, the share in public ownership remains high. Not only do publicly owned companies account for the remaining quarter, but also the Party controls the entire broad administrative apparatus. It controls China's central bank and all of the country's main banks. Also, the Communist Party continues to set targets for economic growth. A few years ago, the target was 8 per cent, but in 2021 it set a less ambitious goal of around 6 per cent. However, the growth target guarantees the Party's popularity among the population. There is an implicit understanding that as long as the Party is able to deliver a good level of growth and continued improvement to living conditions, it is entitled to maintain total control over the political situation in China. Although it is true that there is only one party in China and therefore it does not face any electoral competition, the country's implicit social contract requires economic growth to be sufficiently high to justify its position.

This helps to explain events in China, particularly those since 2008. The global recession and the collapse of international trade in 2008–09 affected China too, and its economic activity declined sharply for the first time in decades. The authorities reacted by increasing "total social financing" growth – a Chinese broad measure of the system's credit and liquidity – from about 25 per cent to above 40 per cent in one year; a similar acceleration was recorded by money in circulation (see Figure 4.1). In short, the Chinese public credit machine began pumping in money and credit as only a centrally controlled economy can.

Figure 4.1 Total social financing and monetary aggregate M2

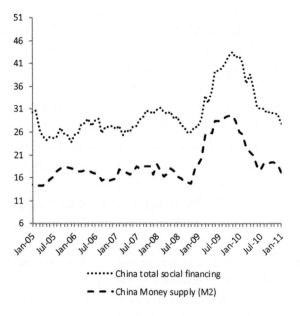

········ China total social financing

━ ━ ·China Money supply (M2)

We have seen that planned economies such as those under communist regimes often rely on monetary and credit expansions. However, strong expansions have problems. In China, private and public enterprises have increased their debt substantially since 2008. Total private debt (households, businesses and public enterprises) grew from just over 100 per cent of GDP in 2008, to 190 per cent of GDP in 2019, and public sector debt virtually doubled (from 27 per cent to about 56 per cent) according to the International Monetary Fund Global Debt Database. Such levels of debt, which certainly have grown further in 2020, create concern.

In any country, even in China, business closures (due to the inability to meet debt repayments) cannot be excluded. Bankruptcies result in banking losses, which weaken the banking system. We have seen that banks are fragile institutions, despite being an important part of the economic system. Any losses will call into question the soundness of banks' balance sheets and induce savers to withdraw their deposits, which can quickly result in bank runs, at which point it is difficult to reverse the course of events and avoid a crisis.

It is clear that a country such as China, with ample resources in the form of official reserves that are strictly controlled from the centre, may be better able than other countries to avoid situations of tension. For instance, in cases of difficulty, it can request stronger banks to take over more fragile ones and, thus, avoid market volatility and bankruptcies. This is feasible as long as there is a sufficient presence of solid banks to cope with the fragility and overuse of debt. Enterprises that have run unproductive investments might find it difficult to repay debts when loans are due and the possibilities of incurring further debt to repay old loans may gradually diminish. In short, at a certain point, there will be a situation of excessive debt, excessive in the sense that it has fulfilled its role in increasing demand and supporting the economy, but perhaps, no longer creates the increased production required for the debt to be sustainable; it is precisely the increased production that allows the debt to be repaid.

This brings us to the nub of the question. How will China stop the accumulation of overall debt (private plus public) and reduce it? The Chinese authorities are well aware of the problem and over the last ten years have tried to contain debt growth. However, unfortunately, they have found themselves unable to achieve this – as a result of the trade tensions with the United States and the recent effects of the pandemic – which has meant that other stimuli have been needed to support industries struggling with the slowdown. But although it might never be the right time to reduce the debt, sooner or later the trend of a larger increase in debt to GDP must be corrected or a crisis will emerge to restore the equilibrium.

A highly-indebted entity is fragile. It may be unable to generate the revenue necessary to repay the large debt. It may be unable to find enough creditors to renew its existing debt and, if existing creditors begin to demand repayments, the entity in question may be forced to declare bankruptcy. If this entity is a bank, then savers' deposits are at risk. Therefore, while debt can be essential to produce value, it can also be the cause of bankruptcy and crisis.

What actions should the country undertake to reduce the growth in the overall debt to GDP ratio? The answer might seem trivial. The indebted entities must reduce expenditure and increase revenue. If increasing revenue (whether from business sales or taxes) is difficult, then all that can be done is contain expenses. However, this implies reducing consumption and investment and, thus, reducing aggregate demand. A reduction in aggregate demand, inevitably, will be accompanied by a reduction in supply and economic activity. In short, a country that wants to contain (and possibly reduce) debt growth in excess of economic activity must accept a certain level of decreased economic growth. The Chinese authorities are sufficiently far-sighted and politically stable to tackle this problem gradually and resolve it within a few years but they will have to accept lower rates of economic growth.

Indeed, for some time now, China's growth has declined from the double-digit rates in the 2000s. It has settled in recent pre-Covid-19 years at around 6 per cent. Obviously, there are many reasons for this slower growth (we have mentioned the trade tensions, but China, also, has moved towards the production of higher technology goods where productivity improvements are more difficult) and it is difficult to isolate the effect of the need to reduce debt levels. So far, China's private and public debt as a share of GDP has not declined, only its growth has slowed. It is clear that the accumulation of debt cannot go on forever and we must expect, at least, a reduction in growth rates, if not a fully-fledged crisis – which is definitely a possibility.

What the Chinese case teaches us is that, even in regimes where politicians are not permanently involved in political campaigning and continually seeking electoral support, the temptation to use monetary and fiscal policies to prop up the economy is strong. The Chinese authorities have been using these means intensively since 2008 to offset external shocks. The accumulated high level of debt is a fragility that the authorities will need to correct, to lessen the risk of a crisis. This correction will be accompanied inevitably by a slowdown in growth. So, will the Chinese social and political systems be able to absorb this slow-down and avoid further repercussions? For the time being, we can say for certain that, even in China, budgetary constraints apply and there is no way around them.

5

Are the advanced
economies different?

"And more than the quality of its institutions, what
distinguishes a developed country from a developing one is the degree of consensus in its politics,
and thus its ability to take actions to secure a better
future despite short-term pain."

Raghuram G. Rajan, *Fault Lines: How Hidden
Fractures Still Threaten the World Economy*

So far, in our exploration of economic policy making,
apart from China which is a special case, I have described
at some length the examples of Argentina, Belarus and
Egypt, whose institutional capabilities and levels of
development are below those of advanced countries.
They demonstrated that in some emerging economies,
with weak institutions, there is a risk that politicians
have too much room for manoeuvre in their management of economic policy. Such examples also show why

developed economies made certain policy decisions such as making the central bank independent or establishing fiscal rules that limit public deficits. To a large extent, it is these precise institutional characteristics that have been built up over time, thanks to the foresight of some politicians and economists, that help to differentiate between advanced and emerging economies. However, it should also be noted, that this distinction between advanced and emerging countries might be in the process of becoming less clear-cut.

In the last few decades, not only have a number of emerging economies achieved high growth rates – China above all others – improving their living standards close to those prevailing in some advanced economies, but also their management of economic policy has progressed. Were the conditions in the advanced countries to deteriorate slightly, convergence would accelerate. An example of a developed country with what many economists consider to be inappropriate economic policy management, is the recent experience of the most advanced economy in the world, namely the United States.

As already highlighted, during the presidency of Donald Trump the tension between economists and politicians has risen sharply. First, Trump's 2016 election, in part, has been represented as a victory over economists, who were accused of not understanding the frustration among a section of the electorate that had been "left behind" in general prosperity of the country, especially those social groups said to have suffered the most from the integration of China and the rest of East Asia into international trade. In fact, most economists believe that advances in technology and automation in production processes in recent years have weighed on the weakness related to workers' incomes in certain sectors of the American economy (see, e.g., Autor & Salomons 2018). To explore this further, we need to assess how the Trump administration has used the main economic levers, namely fiscal policy and international trade policy.

The 2018 fiscal expansion in the United States

Between the end of 2017 and early 2018, the Trump administration introduced a large fiscal stimulus bill that significantly lowered the tax burden of many companies and resulted in a rapid rise in these companies' share prices. The impact on households is more difficult to assess because the lower tax rates (which supposedly benefited mostly higher earners) were offset, in part, by the changes to some exemptions. However, it is likely that the tax reform favoured high-income earners and did not address the serious structural problem of the worsening income distribution observed in the US – if only because it gave tax breaks to firms, whose shareholders are more likely to be higher earners (Krugman 2019).

Most economists agree that Trump's fiscal reform provided a stimulus to the economy at the wrong time, as the US economy was already growing at a rate that was likely above potential. However, they are divided about whether it will be good for growth in the medium term.

There are those who believe that the tax reform has not created substantial additional demand because it has worsened the income distribution and rich people save more of their income and consume less of it compared to poor families; and those who believe that a lower tax rate for higher earners creates incentives for more investment, more production and more employment. In Chapter 3, we explored the fallacious idea that lowering the tax rate can lead to increased economic activity to such a scale as to generate additional revenues that brings the budget back into balance, eventually. This is the idea popularized by Arthur Laffer in the 1970s. Ronald Reagan's attempts to apply it were unsuccessful and, during the Reagan years, the government deficit increased considerably.

Trump's fiscal expansion has similar characteristics to those we have analysed in the context of some emerging countries. It has worsened the public budget deficit (more than 6 per cent in 2019), set public debt back on a growth path from an already very high level (see Figure 5.1; Congressional Budget Office 2020), stimulated demand excessively, which (as the examples of emerging countries show) tends to create inflation. In the US case, it has not increased consumer inflation particularly, but has increased the value of financial assets and housing, and widened the trade deficit by stimulating imports (see Figure 5.2). A fundamental difference from some emerging countries with less democratic political systems, is that the absolute grip on the economy that the Trump administration enjoyed in its first two years of office was lost immediately after the November 2018 mid-term elections

Figure 5.1 US government budget deficit and debt (% of GDP) (annual data, 2000–19) Source: IMF, WEO.

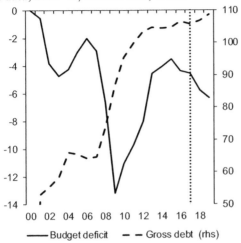

Figure 5.2 US trade deficit (% of GDP) and real estate prices (annual data, 2000–19) Source: IMF, WEO; Federal Housing Finance Agency.

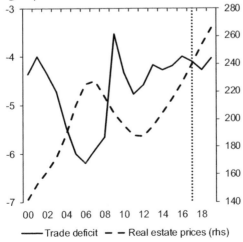

(which ended the Republican Party's control of the House of Representatives). The US economy is sufficiently strong and vital to withstand a few years of unsustainable policies, but correcting them will mean that, once again, certain sections of the population will experience diminished living standards. I would imagine, as the result of more and higher taxes, rather than higher inflation. This will be required to ensure that the budget constraint is respected.

Protectionism

Although important, monetary and fiscal policies are not the only means available to governments to support economic activity or, at least, to satisfy those interest groups closest to the politicians.

The Trump administration was an immediate critic of international trade rules and immigration policies. While it managed to do less than it would have liked in relation to the latter aspect, it did impose import tariffs on a number of goods and, in particular, goods from China. There are many reasons for this choice. Recent US foreign policy strategy considers China to be a geopolitical adversary, competing for world economic supremacy, and seeks to counter it in various ways, including a targeted trade war. In addition, the administration was hopeful that these tariffs would contain the negative impact of the fiscal stimulus on the trade balance, since although the stimulus works to increase imports, these additional import duties will work to reduce them. Also, these import tariffs represent a source of revenue which should help to limit the budget deficit growth.

Nevertheless, economists generally have been in disagreement with the US administration's protectionist measures. Most argue that international trade free of constraints can only bring aggregate benefits for all, because each country is free to concentrate its production where it has higher productivity and can produce at lower costs, and import what is not produced at home. It is a matter, merely, of redistributing these benefits to compensate those damaged by free trade. For example, it would not be worth producing steel in Detroit if it was available, at a lower price, from China. If the United States were to spend less on producing steel by buying it from China, it would have more available to spend for example on education, care for the elderly, etc. What matters is ensuring that the steelworkers in Detroit who have lost their jobs are protected (supported financially, relocated, retrained, etc.). This might seem not to be too difficult, but this social support has not been forthcoming.

Moreover, trade protectionism is being used to support certain groups of voters (e.g. the steel producers) without the US administration having to spend any money. Financing an increase in public spending by raising some taxes would be inconvenient but necessary, since the reduction in taxation referred to above had already increased the budget deficit significantly, leaving little fiscal space to support industries in crisis or to relocate workers. So, who should pay for interventions supporting those areas that, in Trump's narrative, have been the most affected by the effects of international trade? The president had counted on foreigners to pay for them.

However, imposing tariffs on imports does not mean that only foreign producers pay. The intention is to introduce a wedge (the tariff) to increase the domestic price above the one prevailing on the international market. This implies that imports become more expensive than without the tariff and will diminish; domestic producers can increase their production to compensate for the reduced imports.

How much domestic production increases, following the imposition of an import duty, depends on how the domestic producers respond to the import price increase. In the US case, if they were to increase their output to satisfy the domestic demand at a competitive price, then, in theory, the domestic price could remain unchanged at the level prevailing in the international market before the introduction of the tariff and domestic output could increase. However, this could not happen; had domestic producers been able to produce large quantities at low prices, there would have been no need to import steel from China. The fact is that US steel is less competitive than Chinese steel and, therefore, the price of the domestically produced steel has to be higher than the international one. Therefore, an increase in domestic prices due to the tariff is inevitable and will weigh on all activities using the goods on which the duty has been imposed.

Again, the price increase of steel closes the loop and allows the budget constraint to be satisfied. The support to steel producers, ultimately, is paid by American consumers in the form of higher steel prices. In short, to avoid a transparent form of subsidy, financed by an increase in taxes (which, among other things, would challenge the rhetoric about lower taxes), the administration has imposed a higher cost (higher steel prices) on the whole of US society, in an attempt to favour an interest group relevant to the election. You can see why economists might disagree with politically motivated economic policy making.

Crisis and recessions in advanced countries

It is clear that, even in advanced countries, such as the United States, politicians sometimes seek to stimulate the economy in order to increase their chances of re-election. This is what Trump tried to do. Even so, the reader might be wondering what is wrong with stimulating the economy?

The reason is simple and has been discussed in the examples presented previously. If the economy is stimulated beyond its natural capacity to produce (what economists call "potential"), the likelihood of a recession increases. In fact, the imbalances generated by excessive stimulation will tend to correct themselves. If the stimulus has generated demand that is in excess of what the production system can satisfy, then this will result in an upward pressure on prices and/or excessive increases in imports (with a corresponding increase in the trade deficit). The central bank will try to counter these effects by raising interest rates. That is, it tries to cool demand to bring it back to close to the value of supply. In advanced countries, around two-thirds of the economic recessions that have occurred since 1960 have been due to monetary policy trying to counteract rising inflation (Blanchard *et al.* 2015). Traditionally, therefore, excessive stimuli in advanced countries, even if they do not lead to crisis, generally still produce a recession.*

In the case of the United States during the Trump administration, neither the fiscal stimulus, which increased demand, nor the imposition of import duties, which increased import prices, led to a recession. They did put some upward (albeit limited) pressure on prices. The sectors where this upward pressure seems to have been the greatest are in financial and real estate assets. Some excess demand has also been satisfied by imports, leading to a further widening of the trade balance. The Covid-19 pandemic struck before these dynamics could unfold, putting on hold the upward price pressures and the strong domestic demand.

It is important to underline that, even those adjustments that occur in relation to a "normal" recession rather than the deep crises analysed in previous chapters, tend to inflict the most damage on the weaker segments of the population. In fact, during recessions unemployment usually increases more for workers with lower levels

---

* It is worth recalling the experience of some European countries, such as Cyprus, Greece, Ireland, Portugal, and Spain, which saw excessive fiscal or credit expansion during the pre-2008 boom years and, subsequently, found themselves in situations of severe crisis, which were necessary to correct the previously accumulated imbalances.

of education and for ethnic minorities. The families of unemployed individuals may fall into poverty, with permanent negative effects especially on their younger members (Rosengren 2018). The recent Covid-19 recession, although very special in its nature, also follows this pattern.

Any correction to restore balance tends to harm vulnerable groups even if there is no recession or crisis. In advanced economies, it is often the case that excessive fiscal stimuli can be corrected before they lead to serious problems or crises. If a fiscal expansion is excessive and, for example, puts the sustainability of the public finances at risk, then economic policy-makers may decide to correct the policy. Such a situation is rare – the 1989–93 US president, George H. W. Bush's famous phrase "Read my lips: no new taxes" is one case, as his administration eventually had to increase taxes to reduce the budget deficit. We have already discussed the reasons for this, no politician wants to back down in front of the voters. However, in the past, many advanced countries have made budgetary adjustments to put their public accounts in order (International Monetary Fund 2010), but, in most cases, it has been the middle classes and the vulnerable groups in society that have paid the bill.

A budget adjustment can be achieved by either cutting expenses or increasing taxes. If the adjustment occurs during a recession, the most frequent scenario, raising taxes is difficult because people's incomes are already weakened. Therefore, the choice, usually, is to cut public spending on pensions, public-sector wages, education and healthcare. Acting on these expenditures contains domestic demand, which might be necessary to reduce the trade deficit without weighing directly on productive activities that are needed to support the potential recovery. It is clear that the part of the population that depends most on this type of public expenditure is the least well-protected: elderly people (pensions), sick people (healthcare), families (education) and middle-income earners. In contrast, if the economy is flourishing, fiscal adjustments can be postponed, which is politically more convenient. Thus, whichever way one looks at it, fiscal or monetary corrections, due to excessive stimulus, usually are paid for by the lower social classes.

Some readers might argue, here, that fiscal and monetary stimuli are welcome in this economic phase of economic recovery. In the United States, for example, wages had risen slightly even before the Covid-19 recession, despite unemployment being at an all-time low, and inflation is expected to remain contained for an extended period of time. So why should policy-makers consider suspending or reversing the stimuli? We discuss this in the next section.

Do low inflation and negative rates change the picture?

In the last few years, inflation in advanced economies has been particularly low. Before the Covid-19 recession, although unemployment reached historically low levels, wages had been rising moderately and inflation was only mildly affected. I should start by pointing out that it is not easy to assess whether a country has reached the peak of its productive capacity. It is true that, in the United States, standard measures indicate that unemployment was around 3.7 per cent in 2019, but if part-time workers and casual workers are included, unemployment was over 7 per cent (US Bureau of Labor Statistics data). So, overall, the US economy was close to its production potential, although there still might have been some available excess capacity.

More fundamentally, the evidence suggests that, today, wages and inflation react less strongly to domestic economic activity than in the past.* The retail distribution structure is changing as a result of online trade and more intensive use of technology, so the configuration of the margins is changing; value chains are global, so prices are affected less by domestic cost elements; mechanization is increasing and reducing the share of labour in value added while also decreasing the impact of wage developments on prices; and workers' preferences are shifting towards more flexible and part-time jobs in exchange for more moderate wages. All these factors have kept inflation low.

However, this applies particularly to consumer inflation and advanced economies. There are many emerging countries, for example, that have a history of high and volatile inflation (Argentina and Turkey tend to stand out, but the list is long). In addition, if the excess spending capacity due to fiscal and monetary stimuli does not increase wages

---

* See, for example, Gilchrist & Zakrajsek 2019, among the many contributions on this issue.

or consumer inflation, it must be emerging in the form of excessive increases in the value of financial assets (including housing) and/or excessive imports and trade balance deficits. Figures 5.1 and 5.2 show that this is exactly what was happening in the United States up to the end of 2019. While the pandemic crisis has changed these dynamics for a few months, the monetary and fiscal stimuli introduced in the spring of 2020 have reinforced these trends. In both cases, these imbalances will need sooner or later to be corrected.

This situation has arisen amidst extremely expansive monetary policies in recent years. Since the 2008 financial crisis, central banks using various instruments (the best known being quantitative easing – the purchase of long-term bonds) have greatly increased the monetary base and the liquidity in the system. The central banks' aim was to raise inflation close to the target level (usually 2 per cent), a goal that has yet to be achieved. Faced with this weak, if not absent inflation, some critics argue that central banks have room to expand monetary policy further, to keep interest rates even lower (although in some countries they are already negative) and to further increase liquidity.

With interest rates at zero or even negative levels, it is clear that the cost of servicing debt, including public debt, also is falling. This means that states can incur more debt without increasing expenditure on interest significantly. This is true: low or negative interest rates certainly make the public budget constraint less stringent, but it does not mean that the constraint does not exist. It implies, simply, that expenditure on interest will be lower and this will make higher debt levels more sustainable. In short, low interest rates do not invalidate the operation of the budget constraint: they are not a "structural change" to the functioning of the economic system, as some would argue. They are simply low interest rates, which are good for debtors (less so for creditors).

Some commentators might be concerned about these ultra-expansive policies, and especially budgetary policies. The uncertainty is that, if interest rates were to rise without warning, then debts that seemed sustainable might no longer be so. I do not believe that there are strong grounds for this concern, at least for advanced economies that maintain the independence of their central banks. Interest rates tend to rise for two reasons. First, if inflation rises as a result of increased growth. This scenario should not cause concern because increased growth implies more available resources, more tax revenues, and therefore, would leave debt sustainability more or less unchanged, despite the higher interest rates. Second, and linked to the possibility that inflation rises in a persistent manner, as might happen in a post-pandemic growth surge, leading to an upward revision in future inflation expectations. This might force central banks to tighten monetary policy (increasing real interest rates) in order to avoid price increases getting out of control. In this case, there would be two opposite effects: the first, higher unexpected inflation, which would reduce the real return on existing debt. The second, higher future real interests, which would increase the cost of rolling over existing debt and issuing new debt. But while the first effect (the inflation surprise) is usually limited in size and duration, the second effect (increase in real interest rates) tends to be more persistent and have a larger effect on the debt dynamics. Therefore, on balance the increase in inflation may create additional problems for the ability of countries to service their public debt. However, and that's everybody's hope, inflation is unlikely to become excessive and trigger reactions from the central banks as long as monetary policy remains independent and credible in fulfilling its mandate to maintain stable inflation (Borio *et al.* 2019). In this case, inflation expectations would remain anchored at the central banks' target level, therefore rendering their interventions unnecessary. This is the power of credibility: achieve results without action!

The remaining possibility is that the interest rate may rise because the country in question has increased its debt to such an extent that its ability to repay is in question. This would increase the so-called risk premium, not the risk-free interest rate, although this raises another issue since it would mean that – despite low interest rates – the country has become so indebted that this is threatening respect of the budgetary constraint, that is, the sustainability of its debt. The real risk at that stage is that politicians and voters will feel entitled to limit central bank independence because they are convinced that inflation is dead and money can be printed freely. As I showed in Chapter 2, there are limits to how much money can be printed in a given country at a given time. If independence were to be reconsidered and the central bank became subject to political power with the aim of printing money to meet politicians' spending needs, it would not be difficult to predict that inflation would immediately emerge. This applies to the case of many emerging economies. In this scenario, in order to contain inflation, it would be necessary to increase real interest rates continuously and, especially where the central bank has poor credibility – as demonstrated in the case of Argentina – to a point where it would also probably cause a recession. Then, high real interest rates combined with recession would change the assessment of debt sustainability. Higher interest expenditure and lower tax revenues, as a result of the recession, would make debt difficult to sustain, lead to investor flight, an increased risk premium and, ultimately, a probable debt crisis. In short, the budget constraint would again regain the upper hand.

To conclude, weak inflation, which allows an expansive monetary policy and low interest rates, is a good thing, because it facilitates higher debt without its weight becoming unsustainable. On the other hand, if we were to treat low inflation as an opportunity to take command of the printing press and, thus, to compromise the independence of central banks, then this would be a huge risk. We should be under no illusions: a structural change to monetary policy management that reduced the independence of the central bank (as some have proposed), would have only a one-way effect on inflation expectations and, therefore, on inflation trends. The governor of South Africa's central bank, Lesetja Kganyago, described such a situation using an enlightening example:

If you build a maximum-security prison and no one manages to escape, does that show that there was no need to build such a secure prison? On the contrary, I think it shows that it has been well built. The same applies to inflation. Price stability is proof of the success of an independent central bank, not an argument for its abolition. I am concerned that there is a new generation of politicians in advanced economies who have never experienced inflation, and therefore will not appreciate this subtlety. (Kganyago 2019)

6

Italy: the sick man of Europe

"Our politicians? They are like ancient country nobles who, in order to hang onto their luxury lifestyles, mortgage the castle."

Beniamino Andreatta, July 1991

As we have seen, different approaches and contrasting views of politicians and economists characterize both emerging economies and advanced countries. I would point out that, in my analysis, I have been obliged to simplify a great deal, and to highlight certain important points such as the existence of constraints linked to available resources, which, to be sustainable, any economic policy must respect. Otherwise, the budgetary constraint will take over and will be enforced by a recession or crisis, even if it might take a long time before an unsustainable position is reached.

The examples I have given are somewhat extreme, but many of their characteristics apply to other countries. For example, the post-2008 Spanish crisis, which I touched on in Chapter 2, is a case of excessive credit expansion that financed the construction sector. This is not so different from the case I discussed in the context of Belarus, although it is more complicated, because the strong credit expansion was determined not by an explicit choice of the Spanish authorities (as was the case in Belarus) but by an excessive inflow of capital from abroad. The fault of the Spanish authorities was that they did not do enough to contain the credit boom.

In short, my reasoning applies, to varying degrees, to the advanced countries as well. An interesting case of an advanced country where, in the recent past, politicians have indicated an intention to circumvent the budget constraint, is Italy. Since the end of the 1990s, Italy's growth has been dismal. The country suffered particularly badly from the 2008–09 global crisis and, in 2011–12, found itself at the epicentre of the European sovereign debt crisis. In recent years, Italy's persistent economic difficulties have favoured the emergence of forces with populist connotations, such as the Northern League and the 5-Star Movement, which came to power in a coalition government in spring 2018. These political forces claimed that it was necessary to increase the budget deficit, that it might be better to leave the European Monetary Union and reintroduce monetary independence, and that free trade agreements could be disadvantageous. Many economists considered these proposals inadequate. To understand why, some clarifications are needed.

Despite the difficulties experienced over the last 20 years, Italy remains an important industrial country and, above all, a rich country. For example, Italian residents hold €3 trillion in foreign assets (financial assets, productive assets, property, etc.), around half of which are portfolio investments. In financial assets alone, Italian residents hold foreign assets equal to about 80 per cent of national GDP. These are significant figures and give a sense of the country's degree of integration into the European and international financial systems. This is especially significant since a similar amount comes from non-residents or, rather, non-residents hold Italian assets of equivalent value. In short, Italy has a substantially balanced net asset position vis-à-vis foreign countries. Moreover, in recent years, Italy has achieved a trade balance surplus, which has allowed it to accumulate more external assets, year after year. These facts could lead to many considerations, but, here, I would underline only that these data are an indication of a situation of equilibrium, at least with respect to the rest of the world.

The case of public debt is different. Figure 6.1 shows that at almost 160 per cent of GDP in 2020, the public debt is very high even in a historical perspective. It is higher than during the Second World War and it is at the levels prevailing between 1919 and 1924, when it grew exponentially due to strong postwar public spending (which was at the root of the strong postwar inflation).

One of the reasons for this fragility is that about a third of the government bonds issued on the market (about €700 billion) are held by non-residents. Were they to decide to sell these securities forcing residents to buy them back, where would these residents find the resources?

One possibility would be for residents to sell an equal amount of foreign assets. After all, with a balanced capital position vis-à-vis abroad, Italian residents hold foreign financial assets of equal value to those debts. However, Italian savers and investors are not so very different from non-resident savers and investors and, therefore, it is not clear why they would disinvest their foreign savings to buy Italian government bonds, if they were considered risky.

Figure 6.1 Italy's public debt (% of GDP) (annual data, 1861–2020)

Source: Bank of Italy and ISTAT data.

So, there is an important difference between some of our earlier examples and the Italian case, namely that Italy has a substantially balanced foreign asset position whereas the other cases discussed in the book (including the United

States) have or have had a strongly negative position. In the light of this, let's now consider two of the key economic policy proposals of the Italian populist parties: (1) Italy's participation in the euro – a theme dear to the Northern League – and (2) whether restructuring public debt is an option – something the 5 Star Movement has considered. As we shall see, both proposals are linked in part.

Leave the eurozone?

The proponents of a euro exit basically want to recover the freedom of printing currency and to continue deficit spending. However, as I have tried to argue, it is not that monetary and/or fiscal autonomy implies total freedom of use. On the contrary, the risk of excessive use and of pushing the country into crisis, as has happened to many countries in the past, cannot be ruled out.

In 1992, Italy faced a crisis linked to the state's excessive indebtedness and devalued the lira considerably, despite having total budgetary autonomy and monetary sovereignty (admittedly partly limited by membership of the European Monetary System – EMS, which bound the lira exchange rate to the D-mark within a predefined band). Italy had experienced years of high inflation due to a continuously expansive fiscal policy. Figure 6.2 shows that the budget deficit was hovering between 9 per cent and 12 per cent of GDP during the 1980s, while the public debt to GDP was rapidly increasing from 56 per cent in 1980 to past 105 per cent in 1992. Figure 6.3 shows that inflation fell from 21 per cent in 1980 to 5 per cent in 1992, but it was still significantly higher than its trading partners. This high inflation had made Italian goods excessively expensive in the international market and had contributed to a significant trade deficit. The lira was overvalued, making Italian government bonds in lira unattractive to investors, as they feared the possibility that Italy would have to exit the exchange rate agreement and devalue the currency – which indeed happened in the summer of 1992.

Figure 6.2   Italy's budget deficit and public debt (% of GDP) (annual data, 1978–98)

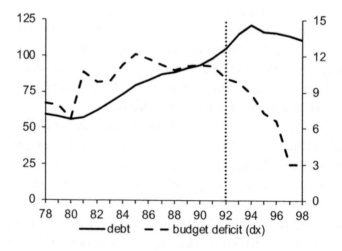

Source: Bank of Italy and ISTAT data.

It was due only to the determination of the Italian authorities following the 1992 devaluation that inflation did not rise out of control. However, the costs of the devaluation in terms of income distribution were evident and not small. The famous "income policy" applied after 1992 to contain inflation, compressed the real incomes of employees, while entrepreneurs in Northern Italy benefited and increased their exports. All income distribution indicators show that inequality increased in those years (Brandolini *et al*. 2018). The higher costs of the crisis and the devaluation weighed on employees, pensioners and the vulnerable groups in society.

Figure 6.3 Italy's exchange rate, lira against the German mark and inflation (annual data, 1978–98).

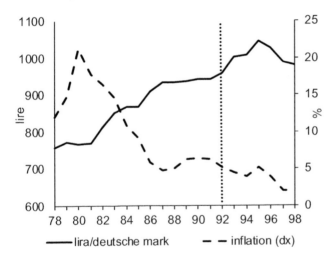

Source: Bank of Italy and ISTAT data.

The experience of those years convinced the Italian authorities that joining the euro and adhering to the accompanying fiscal rules would impose the required discipline over the conduct of monetary and fiscal policies that the Italian political class, on its own, was unable to achieve. This choice was made with the awareness of the limits that governments must respect even if they have budgetary and monetary policy autonomy.

A return to the lira, even ignoring the enormous transition costs, would not solve the fundamental issues, because monetary and fiscal policies are not magic wands that empower the country to grow indefinitely. If they were, one might wonder why countries with monetary autonomy do not grow at higher rates than others over the long term. Economic research shows that countries' long-term growth is independent of the exchange rate regime (see, e.g., Ghosh *et al.* 1996). This should not come as a surprise, especially in light of the discussion in this book of the fact that monetary and fiscal policies can intervene to support the economy in recessionary phases, but are not appropriate for increasing economic growth rates in a stable manner.

So, this is another battleground for the politicians and economists, and between those who would like to regain fiscal and monetary autonomy (populist politicians) and the freedom, they think, to violate the budget constraint, and those (economists) who know that the budget constraint, ultimately, must always be respected. The budget constraint is not consistent with the idea of overstimulating the economy. Unfortunately (for politicians), the main way to improve the economic conditions of their citizens is to increase productive capacity through policies that increase education, research, investment and the ability for businesses to grow. In short, all these measures have little to do with macroeconomic policies and their effects tend to emerge in the medium to long term.

Is debt restructuring an option for Italy?

We now come to the other possibility, however extreme, that, from time to time, politicians advocate avoidance of the budgetary constraint and making others pay the costs of their excesses, possibly by defaulting (or more commonly restructuring) the public debt. In this way, they hope to avoid having to cut spending and/or raising taxes, which are politically unpopular choices. In Chapter 4, we discussed this in relation to Argentina; we now apply the same arguments to Italy.

From time to time, proposals to restructure Italian debt resurface, for example, in spring 2018, during the League and the 5 Star Movement negotiations over the formation of the government and also in the autumn of 2020 in the midst of the pandemic, when it was proposed that the European Central Bank should cancel part of the Italian public debt bought as part of the Public Sector Purchase Program (quantitative easing). Discussions of the restructuring of public debt tend to suggest that government bonds are held by rich rentiers. In the Argentine case, the holders of securities included not only US banks but also many small savers, including European savers. However, from Argentina's point of view, it made little difference whether the foreign holders were rich or not, because they were not part of Argentina's electorate.

In the case of Italy, one sometimes gets the impression that such discussions are based on similar assumptions. Why worry about foreign investors? As far as domestic holders are concerned, surely, they are mainly banks and insurance companies and they can bear the loss; they are not small savers. And, in any case, like all investors in financial assets, the holders of public debt have accepted the risk and must be prepared to suffer losses.

Many of these assumptions are wrong. First, some three-quarters of Italy's public debt is held by national entities (see Bank of Italy data on Italian financial accounts), not so much directly by households, but rather by banks, insurance companies, investment funds and pension funds. However, households own bank stocks, shares in investment funds and have savings invested in pension funds, so eventually, a large share of public debt is held directly and indirectly by Italian households.

Another argument heard in this regard is that since most of the public debt is due to Italians themselves, the problem is less serious, which is another incorrect assumption. First, the distinction between domestic and foreign investors is blurred because even a resident investor can decide to disinvest from domestic government bonds and invest in foreign securities (at least as long as there is free movement of capital within Europe). Second, would we want to argue that if a family has savings in government bonds and these savings are wiped out then

nothing changes? The family will have to reduce its standard of living, give up some of the things that, previously,
it could afford, in short, it will be impoverished. The
question then arises, why would sudden impoverishment
of a large part of the Italian population be a sensible
policy? Among other things, there would be no control
over distributive effects of this impoverishment. There
is no certainty that the greatest costs would fall on the
wealthiest families. This is an important point because
it is not necessarily the case that the wealthiest families
are those who hold (directly and indirectly) more government bonds. Small savers who invest their savings in
pension funds, for example, are likely to be more exposed
to Italian government bonds than the successful entrepreneurs who probably hold a good chunk of their assets
abroad.

Would it not be better to tax the income of Italians
little by little, such that the progressive nature of the tax
system is respected and the components of the wealth tax
and the fight against tax evasion are strengthened? In this
way, the debt would be reduced gradually over time. This
would be less costly than debt restructuring, which corresponds to a very high and sudden tax that would deprive
large sections of the population. Of course, although it
would be better, it would also be more expensive politically. Increasing taxes, cutting spending and reducing debt
slowly, provides little electoral advantage – so, why do
it? The result, not infrequent in history, is that a point is
reached where no one is willing to buy government bonds
because no one is convinced that there is the political will

to make the sacrifices necessary to repay them. Also, as we have seen in the case of exchange rate crises, a debt crisis fixes everything in the sense that it restores the budgetary constraint. However, it does this at a high social cost (the impoverishment of families), but allows the politician in power to claim that the fault belongs to the crisis and foreign speculators.

How does a debt crisis develop in practice? If the government fails to renew maturing government bonds, it is forced to repay them. In a short time, all the liquidity in the government's coffers has been used to repay maturing bonds and the Treasury is left without cash to pay pensions and salaries. Then what happens? One option is to default on the debt, that is, stop paying interest and the maturing principal. What might appear to be an alternative, namely the central bank printing money to buy government bonds, is not a real alternative. As we have seen in the previous chapters, while finite and temporary purchases of government bonds by central banks are part of normal operations, massive and repeated purchases, dictated by the need to replenish public accounts on a regular basis, would lead to a change in the expectations of economic operators regarding the independence of the central bank (Sargent 2013) and, at the same time, would generate an injection of liquidity that would likely create inflation. Inflation is essentially a tax that reduces the real value of both money and securities such as government bonds.

In the case of a declared default, this involves informing the holders of the government bonds that they will not see (all) of their money. Thus, we enter a new world where, suddenly, we are excluded from international financial circuits because all of the creditors of the state (and of other private national entities who are in trouble) will put in place all the measures at their disposal, including legal ones, to recover their money. The state will no longer be able to get into debt and issue debt securities on the market, so it will have to immediately bring the deficit back into balance. All holders of government bonds will suffer heavy losses and a severe economic crisis will be inevitable. The bill will be paid by all those who had savings invested in domestic assets (houses, shares, bonds, including government bonds), because in a crisis, everything loses value; people lose jobs, companies close, and so on.

One might suggest that a country with a primary budget surplus and an external current account surplus, like Italy in 2019, would not need to resort to the market following a default on the public debt (Cottarelli *et al.* 2010). This is because if the default were total (i.e. it reneged on all the public debt), interest expenditure would reduce to zero, so the government would not need to issue more debt because, once the interest expenditure reached zero, it would register a budget surplus (the primary surplus). Similarly, it would not need capital inflows – borrowing from abroad – since a balanced or surplus current account balance of payments implies that the country is able to pay for its imports from its export earnings. In short, the country would have no need to borrow, either internally or externally.

Without going into more detail and to avoid the

discussion becoming too technical, I want, quickly, to refute these points. First, this argument assumes that the primary balance and current account surplus would persist following the default. Now, if Italy had taken that route, it would have been in a very difficult position when facing the pandemic in 2020. Second, no country that has defaulted on its sovereign debt has ever defaulted on its total debt, because creditors are prepared to accept a write off of their claims to the extent that this is necessary to restore the country's ability to pay its debts, but would not be persuaded to go further. This tends to result in limited reductions, rarely exceeding 30 per cent of the debt (Forni *et al*. 2020). This would mean that the budget balance would remain in deficit, because interest expenditure would not be cancelled and perhaps only reduced, although this is not certain because the costs of financing in the market tend to increase after a default. The country is perceived to be riskier (those who have defaulted once will be more likely to default again than countries that have never defaulted) and, therefore, would have to pay a risk premium to investors who chose to buy government bonds.

Moreover, in the past it has tended to be the case that the defaulting country has simultaneously faced severe economic crisis (Forni *et al*. 2020). This is because default creates numerous problems, for example, for banks holding government bonds, their assets and their ability to make credit are reduced, creating a credit restriction. Also, banks may find themselves under pressure from foreign creditors, who are uncertain about whether their claims will be repaid because of the difficulties that a default causes to banks' balance sheets and their ability to repay debts. So, it is true that, with a trade surplus the country would not need to take on new debts abroad, but it might have problems renewing those that fall due.

In turn, recession reduces government tax revenues. What was previously a budget surplus can quickly become a deficit. At that point, not being able to get into debt means having to cut spending or raise taxes, that is, imposing a restrictive fiscal policy during an economic crisis.

This brief description of what a default or restructuring on public debt entails shows why this option is almost never the result of rational choice. On the contrary, it is often the result of the political unwillingness to implement policies that would meet the budget constraint in less costly ways, simply because those policies are perceived as very unpopular with voters.

The Greek spectrum

When we talk about leaving the euro or debt restructuring, the experience of Greece in recent years immediately comes to mind. In 2012 Greece went through significant debt restructuring but this failed to resolve the problem and resulted in Greek debt reaching 188 per cent of GDP in 2019, before the Covid-19 recession. Although, overall, the Greek restructuring was quite orderly (and less chaotic than when Argentina defaulted in 2001), it certainly was not effective in reducing the public debt

(Zettelmeyer *et al.* 2013) and, also, left economic growth severely affected.

The Greek experience is worth restating. It shows how, following the 2012 debt restructuring and other interventions in 2015, Greek citizens and the Greek government fluctuated between wanting to leave and wanting to remain in the eurozone. At the end of 2014, the Greek economy had begun to recover after years of crisis. After winning the January 2015 elections, the Syriza party and its leader, the new Prime Minister Alexis Tsipras, decided to hold a national referendum on the conditions being imposed by the financial aid programme (negotiated with the so-called Troika of the European Commission, the IMF and the European Central Bank). The referendum took place on 5 July 2015 and the overwhelming majority of Greece's citizens voted against the conditions imposed by the aid programme. The following weeks were crucial for Greece's future.

As a consequence of the referendum result and in view of the fact that the Greek government clearly had not committed to respecting the agreements with lenders, the European Central Bank was forced not to increase the emergency funding to Greek banks despite their liquidity problems.* The panic that followed saw queues at the banks as Greek savers tried to withdraw their deposits in euros. This caused the Greek government to close the banks and impose capital controls. Families were able to

---

* See https://www.ecb.europa.eu/press/pr/date/2015/html/pr150628.en.html.

withdraw only a limited number of euros per day and the banks were not allowed to transfer funds abroad. This situation continued until 13 July 2015, when the government reached agreement with its European partners on a new aid programme, following 17 hours of difficult negotiation in Brussels. During those days in July, Greece's government vacillated between remaining inside or leaving the eurozone.

So why did Greece decide to remain in the eurozone? The most convincing argument is that the Greek politicians realized that a euro exit would constitute a leap in the dark, that the consequences had not been fully assessed and the likely costs would be very high. When the banks closed, Greece's citizens began to comprehend what a Grexit might mean: their savings would disappear, their wages and pensions would be paid in a new unknown currency, but certainly not in euros, and the already intense recession would get worse. Without the help of its European partners and the European Central Bank, the Greek banks would be decimated as would Greece's (little) remaining productive activity. The result for the foreseeable future would have been cataclysmic and the Greeks (quite rightly) were afraid.

The Greek experience suggests that, in order to assess their choices, citizens must be able to see evidence of their likely consequences. This is reasonable. They cannot be expected to have an understanding of economics, finance, European treaties and regulations, or to be able to assess how events will develop within different scenarios (e.g. staying within or leaving the eurozone). These issues are complex in many ways. However, having to queue at the bank to try to withdraw savings, was immediate evidence of the seriousness of the situation.

Unfortunately, it seems to be the case that, sometimes, things have to get worse before they get better. That is, in some cases it is necessary for the economic situation to deteriorate further, that is, for the country to go into recession, for people to lose their jobs, for the banks to close, before citizens are able to recognize that the economy is on the wrong path. Is this demanding too much of the citizens? Should they not be protected by the politicians and their avoidance of unrealistic and unsustainable choices?

What can be done?

I hope that, by now, the reader is convinced that the use of both monetary policy and fiscal policy has some limits. In the case of fiscal policy, it is certainly more important to maintain domestic and foreign agents' confidence in the creditworthiness of the state and the country rather than to jeopardize this confidence by imposing sustained increases to the deficit. There are two reasons for this. First, a deficit increase has an expansionary impact only in the year of the increase, not subsequent years. For example, if household disposable income increases (perhaps because of more transfers or lower taxes), consumption and, therefore, production will increase. However, if the deficit remains at this new higher level with no increase in the succeeding years, this expansionary effect on GDP will disappear.

That is, an increase in the deficit has an impact on the level of output, but not on its rate of growth. To influence the growth rate, the deficit would have to increase every year, which, clearly, would be unsustainable.

The second reason is that, eventually, the increased deficit casts doubt on the state's ability to repay its debt and this uncertainty has a negative impact on the economy. Economic agents will wonder whether the government intends, in the future, to raise taxes or to cut spending and may postpone investment plans pending greater clarity. They may wonder, also, if the debt is not on track to increase to the point where it will be difficult to repay it. This uncertainty will require the state to pay a premium on the interest on the public debt to compensate investors for the increased risk related to their securities holdings. These higher financing costs will extend, also, to other economic operators (households and businesses), because any failure of the state is likely to lead to business failures and financial difficulties for households. In short, increasing financing costs will have a negative impact on the whole economy.

So, if reliance on monetary and fiscal policies to increase growth in a sustainable way is unrealistic, then what are the alternatives? What must the Italian economy do to re-stimulate growth? Here, I reflect on a complex issue that involves a multiplicity of aspects. I start with the observation that, every time there is a recession, Covid-19 included, the Italian economy tends to contract more than the other eurozone economies governed by the same monetary policy, and when there is a recovery the Italian economy tends to expand less (see Figure 6.4). This applies to the last 20 years: Italy grew less in the expansionary phase in the early 2000s, fell more during the 2008–09 crisis and, in practical terms, showed no signs of recovery during 2010–11. Also, it fell again and more than other economies, as a result of the sovereign debt crisis, which, because Italy was at the epicentre of this crisis, is not surprising, but its recovery since 2014 was much more tentative than experienced by other countries. And again, it collapsed more than its peers in 2020.

Figure 6.4   GDP of France, Germany, Italy and Spain, 1998–2020 (1998=100)

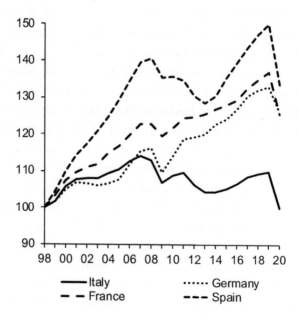

Source: Eurostat.

It should be noted that this pattern (deeper crises and weaker recoveries) is a widespread feature of the Italian economy. It applies to the most dynamic regions (the northeast), to both the manufacturing and service sectors and to value added with or without the public-sector contribution. Italy, evidently, is characterized by weaknesses which mean that if demand falls, the effect is relatively stronger in Italy, and if demand increases, the effect is more contained. It suggests that the Italian economy is slow to react and struggles to introduce the adjustments necessary to defend production when things go wrong. Similarly, when demand increases, Italy seems slow to seize opportunities and takes longer than other countries to adjust to expand production.

When the economy is growing, companies must be quick to expand production and make investments. This requires flexibility to allow increased production capacity, easy access to bank financing to support new investments, labour market availability to expand the workforce and exploitation of new technologies to support these processes. Similarly, when the cycle weakens, production costs need to be contained, market share defended and foreign demand replaced by domestic demand. The lack of these abilities seems to be caused by a series of rigidities that characterize the Italian economy. Some of the possible reasons for these rigidities include lengthy and overly bureaucratic public administration (for example, authorizations for new infrastructure projects take a long time), the family governance structure and management of Italian small and medium enterprises (which hinders growth, deters employment of professional managers and more intensive use of new technologies), the slowness of the judicial system (execution of contracts is a costly and lengthy procedure), the credit system (often reluctant to finance projects with limited collateral) and the limits of the educational system (with low levels of learning and low percentages of college graduates in the population). I may have overlooked some aspects, as for example the role of corruption, but I hope I have made the point that growth relies much more on reforms able to ease the above-mentioned rigidities rather than on transitional support from public spending or monetary easing.

Epilogue: economists and the magic money tree

> "If economists could manage to get themselves thought of as humble, competent people on a level with dentists, that would be splendid."
>
> John Maynard Keynes, *Economic Possibilities for our Grandchildren*, 1930.

Trillions of US dollars have been spent globally to support economies hit by the Covid-19 pandemic. The greatest part of this spending has been financed by government via issuance of government bonds, most of which have been purchased by central banks. This has been truer in advanced economies, where central bankers enjoy more credibility, than in emerging ones, where central banks and economic institutions in general have a less proven track record. Central banks have also increased credit to the private sector, which – thanks also to government sponsored programmes, such as guarantees or moratoria on credit – has grown substantially, especially in Europe. In the US, the expansionary monetary policy has made it easy for firms to issue bonds on the market to bridge the loss of revenues incurred during the pandemic.

The world will exit from the Covid-19 crisis with a certain number of problems, but high on the list will be the increased levels of public and private debts. Leaving aside the thorny issue of the debt of the more fragile and poorer states, which will require official and private creditors to find agreement over some form of write-off and debt relief, this increased debt is not yet a concern. As long as inflation remains subdued and interest rates remain contained, the debt burden, in terms of the cost of servicing this higher debt, should not increase substantially compared to the pre-pandemic levels. The Magic Money Tree however will no longer be so magical, much to the disappointment of policy-makers.

Private debt levels will reach new heights, as will those of public debt. A point will be reached when central banks and commercial banks will not be able to extend much new credit without burdening their balance sheets with significant risks. In Chapter 4 we discussed how potential balance sheet losses would constrain the margin of manoeuvre for central banks. At that point, the Magic Money Tree will cease to exist and the budget constraint will regain its central role. Policy-makers will find themselves in a difficult spot, facing demands for continued fiscal support during the recovery, in addition to the need to finance the necessary investments in health and in the green transition; and having to refinance large amounts of expiring bonds every year and to issue new ones to finance public deficits. At that point, politicians will undoubtedly be very tempted to try to avoid the budget constraint. They will either try to force central banks to keep buying government bonds or will look for other ways of evading it (we have seen a number of examples of how this can be attempted). At that stage, the only way that reckless macroeconomic policies can be prevented from leading countries into recessions and crises is for voters to distinguish between prudent versus unrealistic economic policy proposals. I concede that this is not easy, but I believe that all of us should use our best efforts to judge these important issues.

My main aim in this book has been to emphasize that economic policy, understood as the set of monetary, fiscal and exchange rate measures, can and must help to stabilize the economy. If we decide to use such policy means to enable persistently high national economic growth, then, inevitably, problems will arise. The most appropriate ways to increase national growth potential are unrelated to macroeconomic policies. They instead include improvements to education, labour market integration, environmental protection and health and investing more in research and infrastructure. However, the benefits of these interventions will be seen in the medium-to-long term, that is, well beyond electoral horizons. In contrast, macroeconomic policies aim, mainly, to absorb fluctuations, but they will be sustainable (and therefore worth considering) only if medium-term budgetary constraints are respected. Otherwise, eventually, they will lead to crisis and the losers from an economic crisis are typically the working classes and the less well-protected members of the population.

Respect for (internal and external) budgetary constraints is the cornerstone of good macroeconomic policy, which explains why politicians (not all of them, fortunately) tend to ignore them. For instance, respect for budgetary constraints tends to limit what the politician is able to promise and, thus, circumscribes what the voter can reasonably expect from that politician. Also, it is unclear why voters believe politicians who promise lower taxes and greater expenditure: it should be obvious that, sooner or later, someone will have to pay the bill and the temporary benefits received will have to be repaid, sometimes with a hefty interest. Of course, the individual voter might be hopeful that the cost will be incurred by someone else. This frequently happens and typically that "someone else" is a member of the weaker social classes.

It is unsurprising, therefore, that economics – more strictly, macroeconomics – has been described as the "dismal science". It tends, for the most part, to highlight which constraints must be respected and what can and cannot be done to maintain macroeconomic stability. In some cases, it might indicate better policies than the current ones. One such example in macroeconomics is central bank independence, that we have discussed. But, in general, economic policy, at most, helps to establish a framework and a set of rules to achieve macroeconomic stability, which is an enabling environment to allow society to make scientific and technological advances. Economics research does not make it possible to create new materials or new products, provide new treatments or scientific breakthroughs. These are confined to the fields of engineering, chemistry, medicine and hard sciences more generally. Whereas, economic analysis studies how to produce goods and services efficiently from a limited amount of resources.

It should be clear from the foregoing, that what economics does is to try to understand how to maximize something under one or more budgetary constraints. Therefore, budgetary constraints are a very salient feature of economic science. The family budget constraint determines how much the family can spend, the state budget constraint determines the country's solvency and the national budget constraint reflects the nation's foreign accounts and dependence on foreign citizens. The budget constraint is the absolute foundation of economics and, as such, makes the economy a dismal science because it forces us, always, to reckon based on what we can do rather than what we would like to do.

The current problem we face is that, following three major economic crises (the global crisis in 2008–09, the sovereign debt crisis in Europe in 2011–12 and the Covid-19 recession in 2020), the main advanced countries are experiencing low rates of growth and income distributions that penalize large sections of their populations. As a result, these population segments are demanding greater protection, but, compared to the past, the budgetary constraints are more stringent. When the reality of budget constraints clashes with increasing social and political needs, the result is disagreement and unrest. The conflict between politicians and economists is unlikely to diminish in the coming years.

The current economic situation is substantially different from what advanced countries experienced in the past, especially after the Second World War, when they scored relatively high rates of income growth, often accompanied by sustained inflation rates. The healthy nominal growth added to the state's ability to leverage seignorage, that is, the printing of money by the state to accommodate the increasing demand for money. The latter was due to both rising real activity and to the need to replenish the real value of money eroded by inflation. This resulted in more available resources for everyone to redistribute. Therefore, in the past, in many advanced countries the state could afford to expand public spending on education, pensions, state aid, etc., without experiencing the effect of a budgetary constraint. However, after the 2008–09 recession, growth in the advanced countries has been enfeebled, inflation is low and public debts have risen sharply. The Covid-19 recession has greatly exacerbated these trends. All of which means that the budgetary constraint is now more binding than ever.

The emergence of a budgetary constraint is coinciding with increased voter demand to government for support. The dissatisfaction and sense of uncertainty in large sections of the population have increased greatly in recent years, for many reasons. In addition to the impoverishment of the working classes in advanced economies (OECD 2019), accelerated by the global financial crisis and Covid-19 recession, there seems to be a lack of planning for the future. The reaction to this has been to try to find a welcoming shore, a support, some sort of hope, which is providing politicians with fertile ground for their (unrealistic) promises.

How to escape the conundrum?

From what I have written so far, it would seem that western democracies are in a bit of a pickle. The existence of free and frequent elections requires politicians to be in a permanent state of election campaigning. Enacting policies to prop up the consensus is becoming a daily obsession, which makes it difficult for the politicians to make choices that may cost in the short term but achieve a long-term benefit. China, with its different political system, is much less subject to the political cycle. Some commentators point to the Chinese leaders' capacity to plan for the long term as a crucial element of the country's success.

The political cycle in western democracies is pushing them, to varying degrees of course, towards overactive fiscal and monetary policies that cannot lead to sustainable improvements to living standards. Rather, expansionary fiscal and monetary policies risk jeopardizing people's futures, if they are based on unsustainable assumptions. A classic case is excessive transfers financed by debt, which, sooner or later, will lead to a less generous transfer system to allow this debt to be repaid, that is, a redistribution which favours today's citizens and penalizes tomorrow's. However, those who have not yet been born do not vote!

The discipline of economics tackles these problems with pragmatism. In cases and countries where, for various reasons, the political class is unable to manage monetary and fiscal policies prudently, economists generally suggest the imposition of rules. The first rule, usually, is to make the central bank independent and to give it a clear mandate to achieve stable inflation, thus, eliminating the possibility of politicians printing money excessively to finance public overspending. This represents an attempt to impose a small cost today – forcing sustainable rather than rapidly increasing public expenditure – to achieve greater benefit for the future, namely lasting macroeconomic stability. The alternative would be to compromise the independence of the central bank and the continued printing of new money to finance public expenditure in excess of revenue and increased issuing of public debt for the central bank to buy, thereby undermining both fiscal sustainability and the value of the currency.

Were the central banks' independence to be compromised, economic agents would internalize that the main objective of monetary policy was no longer price stability, but rather financing of the public budget. Such a regime change, if accompanied by excessive and, possibly, unproductive public expenditure, might easily lead to higher inflation. This would mean that the approach adopted by Argentina and other emerging countries could appear viable and, most likely, not even be noticed by most citizens, at least until crisis emerges which disrupts their welfare.

Chapter 2 discussed the potential effects of a central bank that lacks independence. However, it may now be clear to the reader that problems often arise from the politicians' willingness to spend more than they can afford, that is, from their fiscal policy. Limiting a sovereign state's fiscal policy choices is more difficult because there is often no superior (supranational) authority that can impose limits – on the basis, also, of common rules – on the national authority. This superior authority is represented, typically, by monetary unions such as the European Monetary Union. In this case, as discussed in the case of Italy in Chapter 6, the supranational authority can help a country to maintain a certain order in its public finances.

I hope I have shown the reader that the economist often acts like a medical doctor who insists that we must stick to a diet, otherwise we will gain too much weight. The advice of the economist and the doctor seeks to avoid the risk of more serious problems in the future. When economists pronounce about economic policy, often, they are simply highlighting the constraints (so-called "trade-offs") to which the policy must be subject in order to be effective and sustainable. These constraints certainly exist and, I have argued, that sooner or later they will emerge and have effects. Restoring the equilibrium requires someone to pay the bill. That is, some social groups will see their welfare reduced to compensate for the past excesses, if any, produced by unsustainable economic policies. For this reason, economists are not always popular with politicians and, also, to some extent with voters. "If economists could manage to get themselves thought of as humble, competent people on a level with dentists, that would be splendid." Indeed! I hope I've shown in this book why that should be welcomed.

Appendix:
budget constraints

In the following, I will use simple concepts and notation to clarify a few details on the functioning of budgetary constraints.

1. A growing fiscal deficit can be financed by increasing taxes, reducing expenditure or increasing the amount of money in circulation

The government deficit can be written as follows:

$$D_t = C_t^g + I_t^g - T_t + i \cdot (L_t^{bg} + L_t^{cg}) + i^* \cdot E \cdot L_t^{fg} - (M_t - M_{t-1}) \quad (1)$$

where D_t indicates the government deficit at time t. C_t^g are current public expenditures, I_t^g those for investment, while T_t represents the total revenue. The government also has debt that involves interest expenses; L_t^{bg} is the debt of the government to the central bank (for example, with QE of recent years, the central banks of the main countries of the world have purchased large amounts of government bonds); L_t^{cg} is the debt placed with commercial banks, investment funds and the public, that is, the debt not held by the central bank. This debt pays an interest rate equal to i, so that the product between $(L_t^{bg} + L_t^{cg})$ and the sum of the two debts indicates the annual cost of the debt in terms of expenditure for interest (note that the symbol "$\cdot$" indicates the operation of multiplication between two terms). The government usually also issues debt in foreign currency L_t^{fg} whose interest is indicated by i^*. E represents the exchange rate translating the debt issued in foreign currency in the domestic currency. For example, if the debt is issued in dollars and the government deficit is expressed in euros, it represents how many euros it takes to buy a dollar (at the time of writing, it requires fewer euros to buy a dollar). M_t represents the money issued by the central bank and $(M_t - M_{t-1})$ its variation. It basically indicates the share of the deficit that can be financed by the printing of currency ("seigniorage"). In writing the budget constraint in this way we are assuming that the central bank pays its profits to the state coffers, as usually happens even in countries where the central bank is independent.

If the government has a deficit – D_t is positive – it means that expenditure exceeds revenue. All that remains is to finance the difference by borrowing from the market. This can be done either by increasing the debt to the central bank L_t^{bg}, the debt in domestic currency L_t^{cg}, or the debt in foreign currency L_t^{fg}. It is clear that a state can record deficits even for quite long periods of time, but that sooner or later there will be limits to how much debt can be accumulated. Sooner or later, the deficit will have to turn into a surplus to allow the debt to be repaid, or at least it will have to be reduced to zero to prevent the debt from growing. To bring a deficit back to balance, as the constraint written above makes clear, there are only three choices: either you reduce expenses $(C_t^g + I_t^g)$, or you increase revenue T_t, or you print more money $(M_t - M_{t-1})$. In reality, there is a fourth way, which we discussed in Chapter 4, which is to default (i.e. not repay) part of the debt accumulated (L_t^{bg}, L_t^{cg} o L_t^{fg}). Note, however, that the reduction of the deficit that is obtained by not repaying or repaying only in part the accumulated debts is equal to the expense for interest on this debt. Therefore, the annual saving is equal to the lower interest expense that the reduction of the debt by default makes possible.

It should be noted that seigniorage in all advanced countries constitutes a minimum share of revenues. This is because in most countries the demand for money only grows to a limited extent, like the nominal growth of national income. In countries that have tried to use it excessively in the past, inflation rose to high rates. Indeed, if the printing of money exceeds the growth of its demand, it is inevitable that the agents will not want to hold it in large quantities but rather will want to spend it. If the quantity of goods offered does not quickly adjust to the increased demand, inflation is created. When inflation is high, in order to use seigniorage as a source of funding for the government, it is necessary that money growth

$(M_t - M_{t-1})$ also grows at increasing rates. In fact, the real value of $(M_t - M_{t-1})$, that is, the amount of goods that can be bought by printing an additional quantity of money, will be equal to $(M_t - M_{t-1})/P_t$, where P_t represents the average level of prices. Therefore, when prices rise, $(M_t - M_{t-1})$ must also rise so that the real value of seigniorage $(M_t - M_{t-1})/P_t$ remains at least constant. This starts a spiral of inflation and currency printing that in the past has led to various examples of economic crises (Sargent 1982).

This reasoning leads us to an important insight that is often not fully understood. That is, the value of money depends on the government's budgetary constraint being respected without the need to resort too frequently on the printing of money. If a government continues to spend more than its revenues, continuously registers budget deficits and issues too much debt, at a certain point it will become inevitable that part of the deficit will have to be financed by printing more and more money. If this is the case, the growth of the currency will eventually outstrip the growth of its demand and create inflation. Inflation is a way to make all monetary assets expressed in that currency lose value, such as debt securities (even government bonds), but first and foremost currency, because the latter does not pay an interest rate. When inflation is very high, currency has no value.

2. A fiscal deficit is usually accompanied by an external trade deficit

The gross domestic product (GDP) of a country can be written as follows:

$$Y_t = C_t^p + I_t^p + C_t^g + I_t^g + EXP_t - IMP_t \tag{2}$$

Y_t, or GDP is what a country produces in a certain unit of time (e.g. a year, or a quarter). C^p represents domestic private consumption (p), I^p private sector investment, and – as we have already seen – C^g and I^g respectively government consumption and investment expenditure. EXP is exports and IMP is imports. The elements to the right of the equals sign correspond to the various components of demand. Equation (2) simply indicates that the supply of goods and services produced by a country, Y, must be equal to its demand. This demand consists of domestic demand $(C^p + I^p + C^g + I^g)$ which includes demand for domestic goods but also for imported goods, plus foreign demand for domestic goods (EXP). Imports IMP are subtracted by these demand components because imports constitute demand for goods and services produced outside the country, while Y represents only domestic production.

Now, let us define private savings S_t^p as:

$$S_t^p = Y_t - T_t - C_t^p$$

where $Y_t - T_t$ is the disposable income after taxes and C_t^p

157

private consumption.* We define public savings S_t^g as:

$$S_t^g = T_t - C_t^g$$

which corresponds to the current primary deficit (i.e. excluding interest and investment expenditure), but with an inverted sign, of Equation (1).

Equation (2) can be rewritten as follows:

$$(Y_t - T_t - C_t^p) + (T_t - C_t^g) - I_t^p - I_t^g = EXP_t - IMP_t = CA_t$$

where CA_t is the current account of the balance of payments.† Equivalently:

$$S_t^p + S_t^g - I_t^p - I_t^g = EXP_t - IMP_t = CA_t \qquad (3)$$

Equation (3) indicates that private savings, plus public savings, minus private and public domestic investments are equal to the difference between exports and imports, i.e. trade surplus/deficit. With the same level of private savings and investment, an increase in the government's current primary deficit (i.e. a reduction of S_t^g) can only lead to a reduction in the trade surplus or a further deterioration

---

* Note that in order to keep the treatment simple, we are not considering interest on foreign assets held by residents as domestic income. Domestic income should include interest earned on such assets.

† Following the previous note, the current account of the balance of payments should also include interest received from residents on assets held abroad. As mentioned above, for the sake of simplicity, we are overriding this aspect.

in it if it already starts from a negative value. It should be noted that (3) is an accounting equation, and it is therefore always satisfied. The economic mechanisms that may lead to its satisfaction may be different. For example, a classic way in which an increasing public deficit can lead to a worsening of external trade is by stimulating domestic demand which results in increased imports.

3. An external trade deficit implies accumulation of external debt

If a country saves more than it invests domestically, it will have surplus resources that it will invest abroad. If we define ΔF_t as the variation of foreign financial assets, we can write:

$$S_t^p + S_t^g - I_t^p - I_t^g = E_t \cdot \Delta F_t$$

and using Equation (3):

$$E_t \cdot \Delta F_t = EXP_t - IMP_t$$

This means that a trade deficit (i.e. imports in excess of exports) implies a negative change in foreign assets held by residents. Therefore, persistent trade deficits are only possible if there is an accumulation of debt to non-residents. Note that this debt does not have to take the form of bond debt, it can be made up of other forms such as real and equity investments. The fact remains that non-residents increase the rights to the assets of countries with persistent trade deficits.

4.   *A devaluation is necessary when the trade deficit is high and persistent. In order to correct the current account imbalance, the devaluation needs to bring about a depreciation of the Real Exchange Rate. If the government or the private sector hold debts denominated in foreign currency, they may not be able to repay them and thus fail after the devaluation.*

We have seen in the previous point that a trade deficit implies a reduction in external activities or an increase in external debt. When the trade deficit is high and persistent, we reach a point where foreign investors in the country begin to doubt that the country will be able to repay the accumulated debts. To stabilize or reduce its external debt, the country in question will have to reduce its trade deficit (to reduce the speed of accumulation of external debt), or else it will have to reach a balance (to stop the increase in external debt) or finally it will have to reach a trade surplus to begin reducing it (Equation 3).

We have seen in point 2 how a budget deficit (primary current) is accompanied by a trade deficit. One way of reducing the trade deficit would therefore be to reduce the government deficit. This would lead to a contraction in domestic demand and therefore also in imports. An alternative, and generally less painful option for politicians and citizens, is to devalue the exchange rate. In this way, domestic goods become cheaper for foreign buyers, while foreign goods become more expensive in domestic currency for domestic citizens. In short, devaluation changes the relative prices of domestic versus foreign goods, exports increase and imports fall. But a devaluation can be expensive if a country has many debts expressed in foreign currency. Let us take the example of a country where the government is heavily indebted abroad.

If we consider the budgetary constraint of equation (1) and assume that the country in question has no domestic debt, that is to say $L_t^{bg} = L_t^{cg} = 0$, but only foreign debt L_t^{fg}. The budgetary constraint (1) can, therefore, be rewritten as follows:

$$D_t = C_t^g + I_t^g - T_t + i^* \cdot E_t \cdot L_t^{fg} - (M_t - M_{t-1})$$

When the national currency depreciates, or devalues, this is equivalent to an increase of E (for example it will take more euros to buy a dollar) and thus an increase in the value in national currency of the debt in foreign currency. This means that a devaluation (increase of E) will increase the deficit if the government holds debts abroad (or otherwise expressed in foreign currency). We can express the change in the budget deficit following a change in the nominal exchange rate as follows:

$$\Delta D_t = i^* \cdot \Delta E \cdot L_t^{fg} = i^* \cdot \frac{\Delta E_t}{E_t} \cdot E_t \cdot L_t^{fg}$$

and dividing by the level of output Y_t:

$$\frac{\Delta D_t}{Y_t} = i^* \cdot \frac{\Delta E \cdot L_t^{fg}}{Y_t} = i^* \cdot \frac{\Delta E_t}{E_t} \cdot \frac{E_t \cdot L_t^{fg}}{Y_t}$$

If we take the case of a country that has a foreign debt expressed in national currency (that is $\frac{E_t \cdot L_t^{fg}}{Y_t}$) equal to 50 per cent of GDP, with an interest rate $i^* = 10$ per cent and that devalues the currency ($\frac{\Delta E_t}{E_t}$) by 50 per cent, numbers not far for example from the recent situation of Argentina, this implies an increase in the value of the debt ($\frac{\Delta E \cdot L_t^{fg}}{Y_t}$) of 25 per cent of domestic GDP and an increase in the public deficit ($\frac{\Delta D_t}{Y_t}$) of 2.5 per cent of GDP. These numbers can easily send a country into a tailspin, making devaluation in fact an option that simply presages default on foreign debt.

5.   Devaluation creates inflation and reduces the trade deficit. It restores budgetary constraints at the expense of those who pay the inflation tax.

Let us close the loop now. We have seen that persistent public deficits lead to the accumulation of public debt which could lead to an increase in money and inflation (point 1). The budget deficit also leads to deficits in foreign trade (point 2) which imply accumulation of foreign debt (point 3). It is clear that these imbalances – budget and trade deficits – need to be corrected or otherwise sooner or later they will lead to a crisis. Often, as we have argued in the text, politicians do not want or are not able to carry out a correction that would involve a combination of public expenditure reduction and tax increases and let crises correct imbalances and restore the sustainability of budgetary constraints. Typically, as we have seen in the text, crises are of three types: public debt, external debt, banking or a combination of these three. So far, we have not addressed the budgetary constraints of financial operators, such as banks, but it is clear that even in their case they must be satisfied to ensure its operation.

A strong imbalance can be corrected either by restrictive combinations of monetary and fiscal policies (politically costly), or by a devaluation or, at the very least, by a default on public and/or foreign debt. In past crisis situations, devaluation and default often went hand in hand. Both, as I have argued in the text, help re-establishing the budgetary constraint by charging a cost to citizens in terms of lower real incomes (in case of devaluation and inflation), lower savings (in case of default on public debt). Usually, these contractions in incomes and savings lead to a collapse in domestic demand that leads to recessions that in turn lead to an increase in unemployment and thus to further reductions in consumption. In short, a vicious circle from which it is costly to escape.

References

Alesina, A. & A. Drazen 1991. "Why are stabilizations delayed?" *American Economic Review* 81(5): 1170–88.

Alesina, A. & E. Glaeser 2004. *Fighting Poverty in the US and Europe: A World of Difference*. Oxford: Oxford University Press.

Auerbach A. & J. Slemrod 1997. "The economic effects of the Tax Reform Act of 1986". *Journal of Economic Literature* 35(2): 589–632.

Auerbach, A. & Y. Gorodnichenko 2012. "Measuring the output responses to fiscal policy". *American Economic Journal: Economic Policy* 4(2): 1–27.

Autor, D. & A. Salomons 2018. "Is automation labor-displacing: productivity growth, employment, and the labor share". *Brookings Papers on Economic Activity*, Spring, 1–63.

Ball, L., D. Furceri, D. Leigh & P. Loungani 2013. "The distributional effects of fiscal austerity". UN-DESA Working Paper 129. New York: United Nations.

Barro, R. & D. Gordon 1983. "A positive theory of monetary

policy in a natural rate model". *Journal of Political Economy* 91(4): 589–610.

Batini, N., L. Eyraud, L. Forni & A. Weber 2014. "Fiscal multipliers: size, determinants, and use in macroeconomic projections". International Monetary Fund Technical Notes and Manuals No. 2014/04.

Blanchard, O. 2019. "Public debt and low interest rates". *American Economic Review* 109(4): 1197–229.

Blanchard, O., E. Cerutti & L. Summers 2015. "Inflation and activity – two explorations, and their monetary policy implications". In *Inflation and Unemployment in Europe*. ECB Forum on Central Banking, Conference proceedings, 21–23 May 2015, Sintra, Portugal.

Borio, C., P. Disyatat, M. Juselius & P. Rungcharoenkitkul 2019. "Why so low for so long? A long-term view of real interest rates". BIS Working Paper.

Brandolini, A., R. Gambacorta & A. Rosolia 2018. "Inequality amid income stagnation: Italy over the last quarter of a century". Occasional Papers 442, Bank of Italy, Economic Research and International Relations Area.

Congressional Budget Office 2019. *The Budget and Economic Outlook: 2019 to 2029*.

Cottarelli, C., P. Mauro, L. Forni & J. Gottschalk 2010. "Default in today's advanced economies: unnecessary, undesirable, and unlikely". IMF Staff Position Notes 2010/12, International Monetary Fund.

Forni, L., G. Palomba, J. Pereira & C. Richmond 2020. "Sovereign debt restructuring and growth". *Oxford*

Economics Papers. gpaa033, https://doi.org/10.1093/ oep/gpaa033.

Friedman, M. 1970. "The Counter-Revolution in Monetary Theory". Wincott Memorial Lecture, London, 16 September 1970.

Ghosh, A., A.-M. Gulde, J. Ostry & H. Wolf 1996. *Does the Exchange Rate Regime Matter for Inflation and Growth?* Washington, DC: IMF.

Gilchrist, S. & E. Zakrajsek, 2019. "Trade exposure and the evolution of inflation dynamics". Finance and Economics Discussion Series 2019-7, Divisions of Research & Statistics and Monetary Affairs, Federal Reserve Board, Washington, DC.

Giuliani, M. & S. Massari 2018. *It's the Economy, Stupid, Votare in tempo di crisi.* Bologna: Il Mulino.

International Monetary Fund 2010. World Economic Outlook, Chapter 3: "Will it hurt? Macroeconomic effects of fiscal consolidation". October.

International Monetary Fund 2016. Country Report No. 16/168 – UNITED KINGDOM 2016 ARTICLE IV CONSULTATION, June.

International Monetary Fund 2017. Country Report No. 17/409 – ARGENTINA 2017 ARTICLE IV CONSULTATION, December.

International Monetary Fund 2020. Fiscal Monitor, Chapter 2: "Public Investment for the recovery". October.

Kelton, S. 2020. *The Deficit Myth: Modern Monetary Theory and the Birth of the People's Economy*. London: John Murray.

Keynes, J. 1936. *The General Theory of Employment, Interest and Money*. London: Macmillan.

Kydland, F. & E. Prescott 1977. "Rules rather than discretion: the inconsistency of optimal plans". *Journal of Political Economy* 85(3): 473–92.

Krugman, P. 2019. "The Trump tax cut: even worse than you've heard". *New York Times*, 1 January.

Laeven, L. & F. Valencia 2018. "Systemic banking crises revisited". IMF Working Paper 18/206; https://www.imf.org/en/Publications/WP/Issues/2018/09/14/Systemic-Banking-Crises-Revisited-46232.

Lane, P. 2012. "The European sovereign debt crisis." *Journal of Economic Perspectives* 26(3): 49–68.

Mander, B. & E. Moore 2016. "Argentina puts an end to long holdouts saga". *Financial Times*, 22 April.

Musgrave, R. 1959. *The Theory of Public Finance: A Study in Public Economy*. New York: McGraw Hill.

OECD 2019. *Under Pressure: The Squeezed Middle Class*. Paris: OECD Publishing.

Pisani-Ferry, J. 2012. "The great austerity debate". Bruegel, 12 November. https://www.bruegel.org/2012/11/the-great-austerity-debate/.

Posner R. 2009. "Economists on the defensive – Robert Lucas". *The Atlantic*, 9 August 2009; https://www.theatlantic.com/business/archive/2009/08/economists-on-the-defensive-robert-lucas/22979/.

Rajan, R. 2010. *Fault Lines: How Hidden Fractures Still Threaten the World Economy*. Princeton, NJ: Princeton University Press.

Reinhart, C. & K. Rogoff 2009. *This Time Is Different: Eight Centuries of Financial Folly*. Princeton, NJ: Princeton University Press.

Rodrik, D. 2015. *Economics Rules: The Rights and Wrongs of the Dismal Science*. New York: Norton.

Rosengren, E. 2018. "Ethics and economics: making cyclical downturns less severe". 27 June. https://www.bostonfed.org/news-and-events/speeches/2018/ethics-and-economics-making-cyclical-downturns-less-severe.aspx.

Sargent, T. 1982. "The ends of four big inflations". In R. Hall (ed.), *Inflation: Causes and Effects*. Chicago, IL: University of Chicago Press.

Sargent, T. 2013. *Rational Expectations and Inflation*. Third edition. Princeton, NJ: Princeton University Press.

Sturzenegger, F. & J. Zettelmeyer 2007. *Debt Defaults and Lessons from a Decade of Crises*. Cambridge, MA: MIT Press.

Wolf, M. 2018. "China's debt threat: time to rein in the lending boom". *Financial Times*, 25 July.

Wray, L. 2015. *Modern Money Theory: A Primer on*

Macroeconomics for Sovereign Monetary Systems. Second edition. London: Palgrave Macmillan.

Zettelmeyer, J., C. Trebesch & M. Gulati 2013. "The Greek debt restructuring: an autopsy". *Economic Policy* 28(75): 513–63.

Index